JOE McKENZIE

HOW AND WHY CRYPTOCURRENCY HAS TAKEN OVER THE WORLD

Published by
LID Publishing Limited
The Record Hall, Studio 204,
16-16a Baldwins Gardens,
London EC1N 7RJ, UK

524 Broadway, 11th Floor, Suite 08-120,
New York, NY 10012, US

info@lidpublishing.com
www.lidpublishing.com

A member of:

www.businesspublishersroundtable.com

Printed in Great Britain by TJ International
ISBN: 978-1-912555-25-3

Cover and page design: Caroline Li

JOE McKENZIE

MADRID | MEXICO CITY | LONDON
NEW YORK | BUENOS AIRES
BOGOTA | SHANGHAI | NEW DELHI

CONTENTS

CHAPTER 3

THE PRESENT STATUS OF CRYPTOCURRENCY

CHAPTER 4

EXPLORING THE POTENTIAL OF INVESTING IN AN ICO

CHAPTER 5

BLOWING UP CRYPTOCURRENCY

INTRODUCTION

Cryptocurrency is digital financial asset where the holders themselves create value.

Bitcoin, which may be described as the symbol of cryptocurrency, was invented when a paper was released in 2008 in the name of Satoshi Nakamoto. Only known initially by some IT experts, bitcoin had barely any value. But less than ten years later, its value soared as high as 18,000 US dollars (USD) to 1 bitcoin (BTC). The holders of bitcoins achieved the increase in its value by spreading the currency throughout the globe and providing information on its convenience and its very presence.

Roger Ver was an early and well-known investor; he is also known as the bitcoin Jesus, because he used bitcoin and spread the word as he travelled the world when taking part in jiu-jitsu competitions – one of his passions. Gradually, as the convenience and potential came to be known, privately owned stores and other entities began accepting bitcoin payments. This eventually encouraged and led big companies to begin using bitcoin.

Ripple, another key cryptocurrency, achieved recognition when banks and financial institutions worldwide introduced it as a method to transfer currency internationally. While the marketing was different from that for bitcoin, it proved to be extremely effective.

With increased use at financial institutions, the value of Ripple continued to show further growth.

Whether or not the value of a cryptocurrency increases is up to the holder – it is important for them to be personally involved in spreading the word. If you already own cryptocurrency, you should tell people about its presence, its level of convenience and its growth potential. There is still plenty of room for the second or third bitcoin to emerge.

The purpose of this book is to offer knowledge on the birth of cryptocurrency, the structures of blockchains, the challenges faced by cryptocurrency, initial coin offerings (ICOs), and the present and the future of cryptocurrency for people who are interested in investing in cryptocurrency and those who wish to deepen their understanding. The work was written with the aim to promote the cryptocurrency industry as a whole. The first step begins with knowledge, and together with this book's readers, we would like to create a future for cryptocurrency.

The structure of this book is as follows:

Chapter 1 describes what cryptocurrency is.

Chapter 2 presents the story of cryptocurrency, the history of bitcoin and the structure of blockchains.

Chapter 3 explores individual cryptocurrencies and the state of regulations in different countries.

Chapter 4 is about ICOs, which often come up as a topic of discussion.

Chapter 5 looks into the future of cryptocurrency.

Looking back at the history of encryption, we see there was a time when the very existence of codes that governments could not decipher was considered illegal. The use of such codes outside a country or the act of making other governments or organizations use them was seen as an 'export of arms' and could result in severe punishment.

While cryptocurrency's history only began in 2008, at its roots is the fight between cryptography and authority. In the past, there were people who believed that encryption technology would guarantee people's privacy and freedom. The efforts of those who continued to fight have led to the development of blockchains and bitcoin.

It is our wish that cryptocurrency will make people freer and create a better world.

Note that while bitcoin was also called electronic currency in the early stages of its introduction, it is now referred to as cryptocurrency. This is because cryptocurrency is supported by cryptography called blockchains (see Chapter 2). Cryptocurrency is also sometimes called virtual currency. But, as will be explained later, bitcoin and other cryptocurrencies are in no way virtual. To avoid this misunderstanding, this book uses the term cryptocurrency, with the exception of other descriptions contained in some currencies' names, in which case they have been quoted as such.

It is also worth mentioning at this stage that although bitcoins and blockchains are often debated together, and while their relationship is like that of two sides of a coin, they are not the same thing. Bitcoins are a cryptocurrency that were developed with the application of blockchain technology.

CRYPTOCURRENCY GLOSSARY

[altcoin]	Abbreviation for 'alternative coin'; refers to cryptocurrency other than bitcoin.
[bitcoin cash]	Coins that came about from bitcoin for the purpose of resolving its issues.
[bitcoin Jesus]	Roger Ver. He acquired the name when he travelled around the world offering enlightenment on bitcoin.
[blockchain]	Cryptography that supports cryptocurrency. Manipulation is extremely difficult, which makes it possible to secure the reliability of cryptocurrency.
[centralized types of cryptocurrency]	A type of cryptocurrency that has an issuing party. An example is XRP, maintained and managed by Ripple.
[cold wallet]	A method of managing cryptocurrency offline, such as on paper.
[cryptocurrency]	Also called crypto coins.
[distributed types of cryptocurrency]	A type of cryptocurrency that has no issuing party. Bitcoin is one example.
[electronic currency]	Digital currency, also called digital coins or cryptocurrency; one form of alternative currency. Employs cryptography to secure safety of transactions and to control issues.
[exchange]	A matching site for trading cryptocurrency.

[hard fork]	The loss of compatibility between new rules and old rules as a result of changing rules for pertinent cryptocurrency when old rules are ignored and new rules are applied.
[hardware wallet]	A method of managing cryptocurrency offline, such as on a USB.
[ICO]	Abbreviation for initial coin offering, a method for procuring funds. The term was coined to be similar to 'initial public offering (IPO)'.
[legal currency]	Money that is officially determined by governments, such as the US dollar, the euro and the Japanese yen.
[miner]	An individual or operator who mines (see Chapter 2).
[mining]	Approval work for trading cryptocurrency. Cryptocurrency may be received as remuneration.
[moneymaking]	Asset management and savings.
[road map]	A business plan released after the issue of a cryptocurrency by an issuing party who does not initiate an ICO or after an ICO.
[Satoshi Nakamoto]	The person who released a paper that formed the basis of bitcoin. Nothing is known about this person, whether he is Japanese, Japanese-American, an individual or a team, and so forth.
[scalability]	A type of extensibility. Refers to the ability to respond to increases in processing.
[token]	Something like a promissory note distributed to investors at the time of an ICO.
[volatility]	A barometer that shows the variability of the value of assets such as securities.
[wallet]	Similar to a bank account for the storage of cryptocurrency.
[white paper]	A business plan for cryptocurrency at an ICO.

CHAPTER 1

SHOULD YOU INVEST IN CRYPTOCURRENCY?

CAN YOU STILL MAKE MONEY WITH CRYPTOCURRENCY?

It's not too late to make profit with cryptocurrency. You can make a 50 or 100 times profit if you find a good cryptocurrency.

Compared with the history of conventional investments such as securities and real estate, the history of cryptocurrency is extremely short. Cryptocurrency is still in its early days; there is ample room for existing cryptocurrencies to greatly increase in value, and new cryptocurrencies are bound to appear on the scene.

In order to obtain major profits, the key is to identify the cryptocurrency that will increase greatly in value. In other words, you need to develop a discerning eye for choosing a good cryptocurrency. To do that, the three crucial aspects to evaluate are:

- Amount of cryptocurrency issued
- Convenience
- Reliability of the issuing party

Let us first take a look at the amount of cryptocurrency issued. This is one of the major elements for boosting the value of a cryptocurrency.

The maximum amount of a cryptocurrency issued is often predetermined,[1] and so there is a limit to the supply. If demand increases for things that are limited, the market will boost their scarcity (value). In other words, the smaller the amount issued, the higher the volatility[2] of the cryptocurrency will become, meaning that the greater the fluctuation of prices will be.

Taking bitcoins as an example, there is a limit to the number issued, at 21 million. The value (price) of bitcoins soared against the number of people (demand) who wanted to buy and own bitcoins.

Next, in the context of the high rate of convenience, measurements include the speed for transfers to be made, service charges, settlement functions and storage capacities.

In the beginning, bitcoin was excellent as a fast, cheap method for making transfers.

The average service charge for sending bitcoins in around February 2012 was 0.003 BTC. At that time, 1 BTC was approximately 5 USD, so the service charge equated to about 0.0015 USD.

While there have been increases and decreases in the value of bitcoin, they soared steeply in 2017. In December 2017, the highest value of bitcoin was reported at 55.16 BTC (around 1,075,500 USD).

How does the time required to authorize bitcoin trading determine the speed of transfers? The framework for the authorization of trading in blockchains is explained later, but in general, six steps are required to transfer bitcoins. On average, the time required for the first step of authorization is around 60 minutes. Sudden increases in the volume of trade in recent years mean that delays have started to be incurred in this authorization process. As a result, it could take from 30 minutes to, for example, more than 16 hours.

Bitcoin has, therefore, become an expensive and slow method for sending money; it is now necessary to use the past tense and say, "It was highly convenient."

You could previously send bitcoins to the other side of the world in a matter of seconds and barely any service fees would have been incurred. Because of its excellent level of convenience, bitcoin spread throughout the globe. As the degree of recognition for bitcoin continued to increase, so did the number of people who favoured its use, which included numerous business owners.

Emerging among them were also people who accepted payments in bitcoins, chiefly those who operated restaurants, retail shops and hotel businesses. Bitcoin thus became equipped with a settlement function.

The successful uptake of bitcoin by small privately owned businesses as a payment method gradually led to its use by major companies. At present, in some countries, bitcoins can be used to pay utility bills and taxes.

The city of Zug in Switzerland is advanced in its initiatives on cryptocurrency and is also referred to as Crypto Valley. From July 2006, the city started accepting payments[3] in bitcoins for some of its utility charges, up to a limit of 250 USD.

In Japan, there are services being offered such as Coincheck denki (electricity), which employs Coincheck, a bitcoin exchange (to be explained later), and Bitcoin kessai (settlements) by Nichigas, a supplier of energy.

It would have been inconceivable in 2009, when bitcoin came into existence, that such major changes could occur in only a decade.

It is important, however, to recognize when volatility levels are high for a cryptocurrency used for settlements. Let's say, for example, that you purchase 100 USD worth of home appliances with cryptocurrency. You will pay with one coin if a coin has a value of 100 USD. The value of the coin may fluctuate and may drop to 90 USD, or it may rise to 110 USD in value. The fluctuation that the cryptocurrency experiences depends on the general public.

Cryptocurrency is easy to store and use because it is an online or digital currency. You can manage it on your smartphone or your PC. In addition, methods for offline management, such as the cold wallet, have also been developed with the intention of preventing damage by hackers. (These storage methods are discussed in detail later.)

An invention that delivers convenience has the potential to spread around the world. This is completely natural.

The final important aspect is the reliability of the issuing party. There are cryptocurrencies whose issuer is clearly evident.

One such example is Ripple Labs, Inc., which issues and manages Ripple, a cryptocurrency. (The correct encryption currency name is XRP, and it is Ripple that maintains XRP. However, for convenience in this document, it is referred to as Ripple.) Ripple was developed and issued as an international money transfer system. Ripple combines blockchain technology and inter-bank remittance systems. It was launched and is operated as a business that produces revenue by offering a remittance service.

The advantage of knowing the issuing party for a cryptocurrency is that you can refer to the history and track record of the company that issues and manages that cryptocurrency. The issue and management of a cryptocurrency is a business in itself, and so it is necessary to collect and consider information about the business to determine whether it would be a good prospect for investment. Unfortunately, many cryptocurrencies' investors tend to see investing in cryptocurrency as similar to gambling or playing the lottery. Needless to say, the chances of failure will increase if people invest in cryptocurrency casually without conducting ample research.

Thus, when you know who is issuing a cryptocurrency, you should conduct a minimum amount of research on their vision, mission and business plan. This will help you determine whether that business plan is feasible, and whether the history and achievements of the managers suggest they have the potential to support the business plan, in order to judge whether the investment should be made.

It may not be possible to gather all that information. But it is important to make an effort to resolve concerns or doubts when making an investment. A discerning eye for cryptocurrency is nurtured by collecting information and studying and evaluating it on your own. And, to do that, you must first learn in detail what cryptocurrency really is.

WHAT EXACTLY IS CRYPTOCURRENCY?

Cryptocurrency is similar in nature and functions to money (currency). It may be referred to as a digital currency of the Fintech era, or as an international currency that can be used worldwide without any borders.

In this book, money is defined as legal currency. Legal currency refers to currency that is established by law by the government of each country and is only issued by institutions authorized by these governments. A currency has physical entities in the form of bills and coins, and upper limits are established for the volumes issued.

For example, the official name for the British pound is the pound sterling. It is the legal currency that is in circulation in the UK and Northern Ireland (herein referred to as Britain), Crown dependencies and some British overseas territories. In many countries, the central bank monopolizes the right to issue currency notes. Sterling banknotes are issued by the Bank of England. However, historically, in the case of Britain, the Bank of Scotland, the Royal Bank of Scotland, the Clydesdale Bank, the Bank of Ireland, the First Trust Bank, the Northern Bank and the Ulster Bank are also authorized to issue sterling banknotes. Still, these sterling banknotes are not legal currencies in a strict sense, and they cannot be exchanged for foreign currency outside Britain.

The euro is a legal currency that is circulated in 25 countries within Europe, including France, Germany, Italy, Spain and Belgium. The European Central Bank (ECB) has the right to issue euro banknotes.

The US dollar is a legal currency that is circulated in the USA. The US dollar is also called a key currency, because it is stable and reliable and used widely for international commercial transaction payments. Under the Federal Reserve System, the Federal Reserve Board oversees 12 Federal Reserve Banks in key cities in the USA that issue US dollar notes.

The yen is a legal currency issued by the Bank of Japan and is chiefly circulated in Japan. It is not a commonly known fact that in Zimbabwe, the yen is one of the nine legal currencies along with the US dollar, euro and pound sterling.

In these ways, legal currencies are often issued by the central banks of various countries.

'Banknotes' means paper banknotes, and as an example, the banknotes issued by the Bank of Japan are listed on its balance sheet as debts. While this book will not get into a detailed debate about how the balance sheet for a central bank should be, the official position,[4] however, is that banknotes are like certificates of liability for which a nation's bank must secure confidence. This means that banknotes have the same meaning as written acknowledgements of debts. People are living day to day while using promissory notes under the name banknotes.

It may seem strange to shop using IOUs. But the government secures the reliability of its currency by establishing a legal currency under law. It is because of the support derived from that trust that it is possible to convert this to the legal currency of another country, use it to buy goods and services, and use it to pay salaries and remuneration.

Unlike banknotes and coins, cryptocurrency has no physical presence. It is neither issued by a central bank nor established by law. It is digital currency available online, where all trading is compiled as data.

The development of blockchain technology, which is explained later, has made it possible to merge finance with IT. The combination of finance and technology is referred to as Fintech – services for revolutionary settlement, loan and other services that leverage the latest technologies in finance.

Examples of settlement in Fintech are, for example, payment services used throughout the world like PayPal, home accounting apps and accounting software. It is possible to use mobile apps or social media IDs to settle payments without the need to use your bank account.

Loans in Fintech refer to frameworks like crowdfunding, where individuals and companies seek funding online. Crowdfunding may be broken down into two types: one that is an investment, and one that is not investment. With the investment type, you can gain monetary returns like interest and dividends. While there are no returns in the non-investment type, you can obtain finished products and perks. There is also the concept of breaking down the non-investment type to the donation type that produces no returns, and the purchase type, where funds are provided as compensation for products.

These types of settlements and loans are services that have conventionally been supplied by financial institutions such as banks. But the emergence of Fintech has produced an increasing number of companies not related to finance to provide services like payment, transfers, loans and investment, deposits, finance and accounting. This transition has made it possible to see cryptocurrency as a part of the Fintech market.

While legal currencies are established and issued by states and governments under law, cryptocurrencies do not rely on states or governments. They are issued by anonymous individuals, groups or companies.

When using cryptocurrencies to make settlements or fund transfers, there is no need to go through banks or other financial institutions. Thus, as the use of a cryptocurrency increases, so does the possibility to use it under the same conditions elsewhere in the world; it is a tool that boasts an extremely high level of convenience.

For example, you don't need to go to the trouble of getting your money exchanged when you travel or go on a business trip, and you can also use cryptocurrency to remit funds overseas. Think about it: isn't it pretty bothersome to get your money exchanged to the local currency whenever you go on a trip or travel on business? I would prefer, instead of spending time exchanging money, to use the time with my family, for sightseeing or for my work.

There is also the issue of exchange rates. In particular, the exchange rates offered at airports are often not advantageous. Even exchanging money outside the airport does not necessarily mean that you are offered better rates. There may be occasions when you go to a country in the midst of hyperinflation and end up having to carry around increasing numbers of banknotes. There may also be people who are left with unused banknotes after a trip and have nowhere to use them once they have left the country. If more people use cryptocurrency and the scope of its usage expands, all these issues with exchanging money will be eliminated.

There are probably many occasions when individuals or companies need to send money abroad. In particular, those who operate companies that conduct business abroad, those in finance, and families whose members include students studying abroad who need payment for living expenses or tuition fees overseas. Individuals who regularly remit funds abroad may find it troublesome, slow and expensive. The procedures are not only cumbersome, but it also takes days for the money to be received, and the service fees are high. There is nothing good about it.

For some of these individuals, cryptocurrency has already become a convenient method for sending money. Cryptocurrency is sure to be used more widely in the future as a borderless international currency that is common to all countries.

WHAT CAN CRYPTOCURRENCY BE USED FOR?

As already stated, cryptocurrency can be used for settlements (payments), sending money and also for making money. These are the same features as those of legal currency.

It is generally considered that the three functions of money are scale of value, intermediary (exchange), intermediation (settlement), and value storage (preservation). However, I think that the three important functions of money in modern society are settlement, remittance and gains.

Cryptocurrency may be used for buying goods and services by mediated exchanges. This is not different from the general monetary view. But there are no physical banknotes or coins involved in the transaction; instead, these payments are made using apps on smartphones or PCs. There are also debit cards that are compatible with bitcoins and other cryptocurrency payments, which are sold in locations such as Britain, the USA, Hong Kong and Japan. There's the Wirex card, headquartered in the UK, Hong Kong's XAPO card, the US Shift card, Singapore's TenX card, and the Vandle and Manepa cards in Japan.

Service fees, annual maintenance fees, limitations on charges and total credit limits vary from card to card, but the cards are extremely convenient because it's easy to use cryptocurrency for your payments.

'Transfer of funds' refers to what would amount to the domestic and the international remittances at any bank or financial institution. What is different about a transfer of cryptocurrency versus a transfer of legal currency through a financial institution is that you can send and receive cryptocurrencies 24/7 and expect lower charges for the service.

In comparison, and although it may be possible to conduct transfers 24/7 using online banking, receipt of the money will be affected by the hours of operation at the receiving bank and its business days. If you need to initiate these procedures in person at a bank, you have to go to your bank during business hours, and this often has other inconvenient factors associated with it.

While there are also increasing numbers of financial institutions where ATM withdrawals may be made without a fee, it is unlikely that remittance services are offered free of charge. These fees are particularly high when transferring funds abroad; some may consider it an inconvenience to have to pay a service charge each time. But with cryptocurrency, the fees for transferring money are low, although of course there may be high handling fees for some cryptocurrencies, as mentioned earlier, and it will take a while for your transfer to be made.

'Moneymaking' refers to the act of increasing your assets through interest and dividends, which can be achieved by investing and building your savings. Cryptocurrencies gather a great amount of attention with respect to moneymaking.

Currently, cryptocurrencies offer no interest or dividends. Only profit (profit margin) incurred from the difference between the buying and selling price may be obtained. In other words, it is a simple structure where profit may be gained by buying at a low price and selling at a high price.

Bitcoin, for example, has produced many millionaires throughout the world. The profits made vary depending on the amount invested and the timing of the investment, so there are bound to be investors who have gained profits to varying degrees.

When the Bitcoin Market, the world's first online exchange where bitcoins and dollars could be exchanged, came into existence in February 2010, the first trade was conducted at a rate of 8 cents for 1 BTC. In December 2017, that rate increased to 18,000 USD for 1 BTC, an increase of about 225,000 times in a mere eight years. I do not know of any other subjects for investment that have shown such rises in value.

WHERE CAN CRYPTOCURRENCY BE USED?

As stated earlier, bitcoins can be used for online settlements, at physical stores, to send money or for making money.

For example, a website called coinmap (https://coinmap.org) provides listings of physical stores where payments can be made with cryptocurrency. On the site you can search for stores that accept bitcoin payments, using the location information on your smartphone.

There are many stores where bitcoins may be used to shop in the USA and Europe. The range is broad, from privately owned stores to chain stores. For example, in the USA you can pay with bitcoins at restaurants, cafes, major chain stores like Starbucks, and hotels in cities like New York, San Francisco and Los Angeles.

These stores have payment terminals that may be used for bitcoin settlements. They may be the same terminals as those used for credit card settlements, or gadgets like iPads may also be used.

The method of settlement with bitcoins is as follows:

1. Bitcoin is transferred from an exchange to your mobile wallet (cryptocurrency accounts are called wallets), or you download an exchange app on your smartphone.
2. You shop at a store that accepts payments in bitcoins.

You have your wallet read the QR code on the store terminal and complete your payment. It's very easy.

Besides physical stores, an increasing number of online shops, as well the likes of Amazon, are introducing bitcoin payments. Other than these, companies like Microsoft, Expedia, Dish Network (a major satellite broadcaster in the USA), AutoPartsWay (an online shop that specializes in car parts), Gyft (an online gift card shop in the USA) and Bic Camera (a seller of household appliances in Japan) have also incorporated bitcoin payments.

Although not direct settlements, bitcoins may be charged for Visa prepaid cards for use at Visa merchant stores throughout the world. There are approximately 40 million Visa merchant stores in more than 200 countries and regions throughout the globe. Besides Visa prepaid cards, bitcoins may also be used for buying or making charges on Amazon gift cards, V-Preca, Nanaco gift, Edy gift or Net Cash.

Among the numerous cryptocurrencies in existence, bitcoin is the most advanced with regard to its infrastructure for settlement. Additionally, as many cryptocurrencies may be withdrawn in bitcoins, it is also possible to exchange the cryptocurrency that you have for bitcoins and use it for shopping and other purposes.

Impressively, it isn't only companies that offer goods and services that are introducing bitcoin payments. In Germany, for example, Enercity, the biggest energy company supplying electricity and gas in Hannover, has incorporated bitcoin settlements. The system is easy to use, even for beginners: you use the payment code on the invoice to pay the bill. And in Chiasso, Switzerland, it has been possible to pay taxes using bitcoin since 2018.

Payments in bitcoins are gradually spreading, from payments at physical stores and online shops to payments for purchases and charges for prepaid cards and gift cards and to payments for public utilities and taxes.

When sending money, it is possible to use a wallet or an exchange. To be specific, it is possible to send cryptocurrency at your leisure to your family and friends. For example, in 2011 a friend sent me bitcoins when I was paying the bill at a restaurant in the legal currency. I often sent bitcoins to friends and vice versa when I didn't have ample small change. We sent bitcoins as an alternative method of payment. Later, however, when bitcoin's value suddenly began to soar, my friends conversely wanted to start collecting bitcoin.

Moneymaking can be achieved when using a wallet or an exchange in the same way as you would to send money. What you do is store (save) the cryptocurrency that you have obtained through, for example, a purchase in a wallet or an exchange. And when the cryptocurrency's value goes up, you can sell it and make a withdrawal, including the profit made.

In addition to long-term possession, it should also be possible to achieve profit through day trading, where you complete a transaction within the same day, or through swing trading, where you conduct transactions over several days or weeks.

There are cryptocurrencies that fluctuate greatly – i.e. those that have high rates of volatility – and cryptocurrencies that have low levels of fluctuation. With a cryptocurrency with a high rate of volatility, it is possible to conduct day trading or swing trading.

While some individuals only consider long-term investment, how people think about and make money varies from person to person.

WHERE CAN YOU OBTAIN CRYPTOCURRENCY?

There are primarily four methods to obtain cryptocurrency:

- Buying it from cryptocurrency exchanges
- Buying it from a broker
- Having it sent to you directly
- Through mining

The most generic method for an investor to obtain cryptocurrency is buying it from a cryptocurrency exchange.

Cryptocurrency exchanges exist online and are operated by various companies; some are operated by the issuer of a cryptocurrency. Exchanges make available cryptocurrencies that are ready to be bought and sold. An exchange is a place where people who want to buy cryptocurrency and people who want to sell cryptocurrency come together and conduct trade. In other words, an exchange mediates between buyers and sellers. Because of that, exchanges are sometimes called matching sites. But although called sites, they do not actually exist physically somewhere; they exist on the internet.

Also, trade in this context refers to exchanges between legal currencies like the US dollar, the euro and the yen and cryptocurrencies, a certain cryptocurrency or another cryptocurrency.

Trading at an exchange takes place through negotiated transactions. These are not necessarily one-on-one transactions. There are actually many occasions when, depending on the desired volume of trade, the transaction will be one currency versus a multiple number of currencies.

In negotiated transactions, an increase in the number of people who want to buy or own a currency will result in an increase in the value of that cryptocurrency, while an increase in the number of people who want to sell will result in a decrease in value. For that reason, the degree of matching will vary greatly depending on the exchange or the size of the market. Because of that, variances occur in the speed of trading or the price, depending on the exchange, even when you're attempting to trade the same type or the same volume of cryptocurrency.

The fact that a cryptocurrency is traded at numerous exchanges means both advantages and disadvantages for the person in possession of that cryptocurrency. The advantage is that you can select an exchange that is convenient for you to use in view of its service charges and the languages it uses. The disadvantage is that because many holders of cryptocurrencies are scattered around numerous exchanges, it will be difficult to find a match at every exchange.

Next, unlike direct negotiated transactions between cryptocurrency holders at an exchange, buying at a brokerage is a method for purchases at values indicated by the brokerage. There are also brokerages where you need to pay a separate handling charge. When buying cryptocurrency at an exchange, you may sometimes increase the rate when you buy it in a large volume; an advantage of buying at a brokerage is that you can buy at a fixed rate, and the value will not vary. However, sometimes it may be cheaper at times to buy at an exchange, depending on the total amount of your purchase.

The third method is to have the cryptocurrency sent directly to you by someone who is already in possession of cryptocurrency.

As mentioned earlier, you can obtain cryptocurrency in the place of legal currency when, for example, you receive money that a friend owes you. A transaction is complete if both the sender and the recipient acknowledge the value of the particular cryptocurrency being used.

There was a time in the past when my company paid employees' salaries in bitcoins. That time was around 2011 and 2012. It was possible partly due to the fact that price fluctuations for bitcoins had not been as violent as they are now, and because both management and employees recognized its value.

The last method, mining, is unique for obtaining cryptocurrency. While it is fairly easy to understand purchases of cryptocurrency at exchanges and sending it directly, the term mining probably has no meaning unless you have prior knowledge. Thus, details on the method for obtaining cryptocurrency through mining are given later in this book.

WHAT IS A CRYPTOCURRENCY EXCHANGE?

As mentioned earlier, a cryptocurrency exchange is a broker who mediates the buying and selling of cryptocurrency. Although some may think that a cryptocurrency exchange is similar to a stock exchange, there is an error in that understanding. A cryptocurrency exchange is not a market or a venue for trading in the way that a stock exchange serves the securities exchange market; it is a trading brokerage for the market. The work of a cryptocurrency exchange is closer to the work done by securities companies, but when you take a close look at the framework of the actual transactions that are conducted at a cryptocurrency exchange, you will see that it has aspects that resemble those of a foreign exchange (FX) company.

A securities exchange is a stock market that connects investors and shareholders and is set up so that the buying and selling of stocks can be conducted in a smooth manner. The securities firms conduct the trading of stocks at an exchange.

In the investment of stocks, securities companies that receive orders from customers (investors) present those orders at a stock exchange to establish deals within the stock market. Thus, each securities firm mediates buying and selling of stocks. This is the same principle as how an FX company links investors with the FX market.

Incidentally, the proper name for FX (foreign exchange) is foreign exchange margin trading.

With FX, FX companies mediate the buying and selling of currency. Orders are received from customers, and the FX companies present purchase and sales orders from their customers to the FX market and established deals.

In a similar way, cryptocurrency exchanges connect investors with the cryptocurrency market. A cryptocurrency exchange receives purchase and sales orders from customers and presents these to the cryptocurrency market, and a deal is established.

As for sending cryptocurrency, an exchange that receives an order from a customer to send cryptocurrency sends it to the recipient. It is through such flows that a cryptocurrency exchange mediates buying and selling and the transfer of funds.

However, the discussion up to this point has been about the superficial structure. The stories behind the scenes, which are hidden within the framework of transactions at FX companies, will now be explored.

Have you ever heard the term bucketing? It is called *nomi koi* in Japanese, sometimes written using kanji characters that are pronounced to mean 'drinking' or 'indulging in the act of drinking'. The term is said to have been derived from the world of horse races.

Imagine, for example, that you would like to bet on a horse but you're busy with your work and have plans for your personal time and are unable to go out and buy betting slips. Therefore you ask a friend who likes horse races to buy a betting slip for you, and you give him money. The friend doesn't buy you a ticket, thinking that your prediction for a winning horse is wrong anyway, and instead spends it on food and drink. And if your prediction proves not to happen, the money that you've given your friend for buying your betting slip will become profit for him. Such an action is expressed as "drinking or bucketing a betting slip", which is where the term bucketing was derived, and led to those who practise bucketing, or bucketeering, as a trade to be called bucketeers.

As for securities companies, bucketing is forbidden in Japan by the Financial Instruments and Exchange Law (called the Securities and Exchange Act until 2007). It is also illegal in many states of the USA, including California[5] and Washington state[6].

However, the situation varies somewhat at FX companies. For example, most FX companies in Japan employ a trading method called negotiated transactions or use over-the-counter transactions. As the names suggest, these are forms of transactions where direct negotiations are conducted between the buyer and the seller to establish a deal. As a dealer from the FX company mediates, they are also sometimes called dealing-desk methods, which means that the FX company is the counterpart with which the investor conducts the transaction.

When negotiated transaction methods are used, the FX company can make a deal without actually taking the customer's order to the market. It is possible, for example, to directly match customer orders without employing market trading in between. On the other hand, when seen from another standpoint, it would also be seen as leaving room for bucketing. Since there is no law against it, there is no way for the customer to know how their order is being processed at the FX company. Of course, it is important to note that not all FX companies engage in bucketing.

Only a fraction of investors are able to steadily produce big profits through foreign currency investments. It is certain that even if their profits were to be paid, as long as the total amount in losses for investors who have lost money exceeds that, it is more profitable for an FX company to attempt bucketing than to collect handling fees at the time of buying and selling.

Many blogs written by investors about their doubts concerning FX companies can be found by searching the internet. There are also many articles[7] that warn beginners about FX trading.

The signs of an insincere FX company or possible bucketeering may include, for example:

- Sudden rejection when the size of an investment is increased
- A suspicious amount of time taken before a transaction is completed
- Variances occurring in the rate between the time that an order is made and when a transaction is completed

Cryptocurrency exchanges employ similar transaction methods as FX companies. In other words, they have the room to get involved in bucketing. Cryptocurrency exchanges that want to avoid their customers harbouring the type of doubts that they may have with FX companies tend to choose a name that is suggestive of 'securities exchanges' for equities.

In other words, it is important to remember that an exchange for cryptocurrency is essentially a different entity from a securities exchange. Also, because fewer countries have a licensing system, they have less social credibility than securities companies, which are strictly regulated under the laws of each country.

To offer a little supplementary detail on transactions conducted by FX companies, there is also a method of transaction that exists called trading at an exchange market, or no dealing desk (NDD). There are advantages and disadvantages for both the NDD and the dealing desk (DD) methods; needless to say, it is necessary to make a careful examination when selecting an FX company. The following pages provide guidance in choosing a cryptocurrency exchange.

On the other hand, in various countries, efforts are spreading to require cryptocurrency transactions to have some kind of licensing. As of June 2018, however, the USA and Japan are the only two countries that have clearly established such a position.

On 16 July 2014, the New York State Department of Financial Services (NYSDFS) announced BitLicense, a licence system for operators of bitcoin-related businesses, which took effect in August 2015.

BitLicense is a law that concerns bitcoin and other cryptocurrency related to businesses. To be specific, it stipulates by law that a licence is required when exchanging legal currencies with cryptocurrency, sending or receiving cryptocurrency, or managing or issuing cryptocurrency.

It is only the following seven companies that have obtained a licence as of June 2018:[8]

- bitFlyer USA, a US subsidiary of the Japanese company bitFlyer, Inc.
- Coinbase
- Xapo
- Genesis Global Trading, a subsidiary of the Digital Currency Group
- XRPII, a subsidiary of Ripple
- Circle
- Square

BitLicense examinations are extremely strict and complicated, and many companies that had been operating exchanges before the law took effect are said to have given up on obtaining a licence and left the state of New York.[9]

On 7 March 2018, the United States Securities and Exchange Commission (SEC), which monitors and oversees securities trading for equities and government bonds, announced that registration with the SEC will be mandatory for transactions platforms for bitcoins and other digital assets, which made it necessary to register all cryptocurrency transactions with the SEC.[10]

In a statement released in April 2018,[11] the Financial Conduct Authority (FCA) of Britain said that "cryptocurrency is not currently regulated under the FCA" and that "cryptocurrency transactions have the potential of becoming financial instruments". As a result, guidelines pertaining to financial derivatives as stipulated by the FCA and the EU soon followed and clearly stated that companies that conduct futures trading, contracts for differences, and options trading must receive approval from the FCA.

In May 2018, investigations began in Britain into 24 cryptocurrency exchanges that had not received approval.[12] The purpose was to confirm whether these companies were "conducting tasks which should have received approval from the FCA".

In France, the Autorité des Marchés Financiers (AMF) concluded that "cryptocurrency contracts (transactions) conducted with cash settlement may at times be categorized as derivatives, regardless of the legal capacity of cryptocurrency", and as a result it issued a statement that "online platforms (exchanges) which offer cryptocurrency derivatives are applicable as markets in Financial Instruments Directive 2 (MiFID 2: A new law that took effect in January 2018 for the purpose of harmonizing financial and capital markets in EU member states). Thus, exchanges must obtain approval, follow the business code of conduct, and abide by the European Market Infrastructure Regulation (EMIR) obligation to report transactions to agencies where information on transactions are accumulated." The term derivatives refers to a new financial instrument that has been derived from conventional transaction systems for underlying securities for equities, interest, currency and exchanges. This may be seen as a move to align with the trend of a tightening of regulations and keep in line throughout the entire EU region.

The Ministry of Finance of the Russian Federation compiled a bill concerning cryptocurrency transactions and submitted it to the Ministry of Finance of the Russian Federation at the end of 2017. The bill reveals definitions for cryptocurrency, tokens, smart contracts, cryptocurrency exchanges and mining, and stipulates that the public has the right to convert cryptocurrency to other digital assets or inconvertible money.[13,14]

Deputy Finance Minister Alexey Moiseev stated that: "Cryptocurrency transactions will be set as a standard. The concept for that is that it should be bought and sold at an official cryptocurrency exchange, that it would be made legal."[15] What this means is that exchanges would exist by licence in Russia as well. Furthermore, the law came into force on 29 July 2018.[16]

In Japan, the amended Payment Services Act, which took effect in April 2017, led the country to follow the USA in introducing a licence system. Exchanges operated by 11 companies received approval from the Financial Services Agency and were registered on 29 September 2017.

The exchanges that were approved and registered at the time are:

- MONEY PARTNERS CO., LTD.
- QUOINE CORPORATION
- bitFlyer, Inc.
- bitbank, inc.
- SBI Virtual Currencies Co., Ltd.
- GMO Coin, Inc.
- BitTrade Co., Ltd.
- BtcBox co., Ltd.
- BITPoint Japan Co., Ltd.
- Fisco Cryptocurrency Exchange Inc.
- Tech Bureau, Corp. (Zaif)

An additional 19 companies to those listed above were registered as equivalent businesses. An equivalent business is a business that has been conducting the business of exchanging virtual currency prior to the enactment of the law and has begun application procedures with the Financial Services Agency.

In Japan, an exchange that is not registered as a business that operates a virtual currency exchange is prohibited from engaging in legal currency and cryptocurrency transactions. Regulations have also started to be imposed on sales activities in Japan by overseas cryptocurrency exchanges that have not completed registration in Japan. For example, there was a case of an exchange called Kraken (a US-based company) that had been registered as an equivalent operator and which withdrew its application, suspended its services for Japanese residents and became unable to create new accounts.

In Hong Kong, there are no laws at present on licensing for cryptocurrency exchanges. However, the Hong Kong Securities and Futures Commission (HK SFC) has determined that cryptocurrency falls under securities under the Securities and Futures Ordinance. Thus, it is not possible to conduct cryptocurrency transactions without a licence. For example, in February 2018 the commission issued a strong warning to seven exchanges related to Hong Kong not to handle cryptocurrency.[17] Ashley Alder, CEO at the Securities and Futures Commission, also said: "We will continue to monitor the (cryptocurrency) market and initiate regulations if necessary."[18]

Singapore has not only adopted an open-minded attitude on cryptocurrency, but also pushed forward advanced initiatives with regards to blockchains. In March 2018, it was revealed that the Monetary Authority of Singapore (MAS) was considering additional regulations for the purpose of protecting investors.[19] And in May 2018, MAS issued a warning to eight cryptocurrency exchanges to comply with the relevant laws.

Brazil, which is in the midst of an unprecedented cryptocurrency boom, is another country that has no laws to control cryptocurrency. Although in January 2018 there was a minimal move to prohibit funds from buying cryptocurrencies, to date no licensing system exists for exchanges. However, the assembly is said to be moving towards regulating exchanges. When that happens, expectations are that Japan's licensing system for traders of virtual currency exchange will be used as a model.

In different ways, regulations concerning cryptocurrency exchanges are being tightened worldwide, and there is a major trend towards introducing licensing systems.

The backdrop is probably the standpoint of protecting investors from the damage of hackers as well as the standpoint of collecting taxes. There is, naturally, the purpose of preventing acts such as money laundering.

Additionally, it is certain that the safety of investing in cryptocurrency will be boosted if exchanges are made to receive licences from the government. Still, hacking incidents occur that are irrelevant to such licensing systems.

Bearing that in mind, how should investors choose an exchange?

HOW TO CHOOSE A CRYPTOCURRENCY EXCHANGE AND BUY CRYPTOCURRENCY?

There are four points, as follows, that should be checked when choosing an exchange:

- Handling fees
- Types and quantity of cryptocurrencies handled
- Trading volume
- Security

The first item, handling fees, refers to the service charges incurred when buying, selling, sending or withdrawing cryptocurrency. If you want to buy, sell, send or withdraw frequently, you might select an exchange by its low handling fees. Of course, this book does not recommend the idea of choosing an exchange based on the low rates of handling fees alone; you should consider this strictly as a reference point.

The handling fees at major exchanges are:

- **BINANCE:**
  0.015–0.1%
- **Bittrex:**
  0.25%
- **KuCoin:**
  0.1%

- **BitMEX:**
  -0.25–0.25%[20]
- **Huobi:**
  0.2%
- **Kraken:**
  0–0.26%

While the market rate for handling fees for buying and selling varies from country to country, it may be said that these are often set at 0.1–0.15%.

The item "types and quantity of cryptocurrency that is handled" refers to the types of cryptocurrencies that it is possible to trade at an exchange.

A simple assumption is to believe that it would be good to choose an exchange that deals with a large variety of cryptocurrencies. The type of cryptocurrency that you may be interested in buying may not necessarily be traded by every cryptocurrency exchange worldwide. It may be a cryptocurrency that is not traded at major exchanges.

There are ways to distinguish cryptocurrencies for investment by "making considerations with a specific exchange in mind (low handling fees or a large variety of cryptocurrencies traded, etc." or by "considering with a specific cryptocurrency in mind (level of convenience, reliability, future potential)".

Nevertheless, when considering where to invest, it is wise to avoid having a specific cryptocurrency exchange in mind to begin with. The reason for this is that while a major exchange may trade a cryptocurrency, that does not necessarily mean that it is safe. It is hoped that you will carefully choose a cryptocurrency to invest in and then select an exchange.

As a point of reference, the types of cryptocurrencies traded at various cryptocurrency exchanges are as follows (as of July 2018):

- **Binance:**
  More than approximately 120 types of cryptocurrencies
- **Bittrex:**
  More than approximately 200 types of cryptocurrencies
- **KuCoin:**
  More than approximately 100 types of cryptocurrencies
- **BitMEX:**
  Approximately eight types of cryptocurrencies
- **Huobi:**
  More than approximately 100 types of cryptocurrencies
- **Kraken:**
  Approximately 17 types of cryptocurrencies

Trading volume refers to the level of matches that are made. As exchanges are matching sites where people who want to buy cryptocurrencies and those who want to sell assemble, the greater the volume of trading, the greater the volume of matches that will be made. A high level of matches means it will be easy for buying and selling orders to be fulfilled. If trading volume at an exchange is low, a situation will arise where there is no one who will sell when you want to buy, or there is no one who will buy when you want to sell.

Imagine, for example, that you want to sell cryptocurrency equivalent to 10,000 USD in value. You may want to sell at a rate of 10 USD per cryptocurrency coin, but no matches will be made unless you can find people who want to buy at 10 USD per cryptocurrency coin, adding up to a total 10,000 USD. Although you may want to withdraw coins equivalent to 10,000 USD by the next day, it may take a week until matching (selling) is complete. It is possible to avoid such a situation if you choose an exchange that has a large volume of trading.

For reference, the total volume of trading in 24 hours as of 25 July 2018 was as follows:

- **Binance:**
  Approximately 18 billion yen
- **BitRex:**
  Approximately 140 million yen
- **KuCoin:**
  Approximately 34 million yen
- **BitMEX:**
  Approximately 85 billion yen
- **Huobi:**
  Approximately 1.3 billion yen
- **Kraken:**
  Approximately 270 million yen

Finally, security refers to the safety level of an exchange. As mentioned earlier, licences from the supervising authorities have become necessary for cryptocurrency exchanges in the USA and Japan. The number of other countries where a licence system is expected to be introduced is also increasing.

Regardless of licensing, hacking incidents continue to occur. It is evident that licensing does not equal safety. There are probably individuals who say they have failed at investing in a cryptocurrency or that they have experienced damage from hacking. To avoid that happening, the selection of cryptocurrency exchange is critical.

The Mt. Gox incident is a famous hacking incident concerning cryptocurrency. It occurred on 19 June 2011, and more than 750,000 BTC as well as 2.8 billion yen for purchases in the company's bank account disappeared.

There have also been other incidents, such as: the BitFloor incident that occurred in September 2012, 24,000 BTC stolen; the Poloniex incident in March 2014, the precise amount in losses has not been disclosed; the Bitstamp incident on 4 January 2015, 19,000 BTC stolen; and the Bitfinex incident on 2 August 2016, 120,000 BTC stolen.

It is imperative to understand that in all these hacking incidents, the issue was not with the cryptocurrency blockchains themselves but with security issues at the cryptocurrency exchanges instead.

Hacking incidents have also occurred with cryptocurrencies other than bitcoin. For example, in Japan, 5.8 billion yen worth of the cryptocurrency New Economic Movement (NEM) was stolen from the exchange Coincheck in 2018. It happened after Japan's Financial Services Agency implemented its licensing system for exchanges. This means that it is an illusion to believe that an exchange is safe because it is recognized by the government, and that leaving the storage of cryptocurrency up to an exchange alone is high risk.

Among the exchanges are companies that manage cryptocurrencies for all users with a single wallet rather than creating a wallet for each user. Currently, there are many such exchanges. However, in this case, if one wallet is hacked, all the encryption currency in the wallet will be stolen. This is an extremely sloppy management system. It would be better to have an exchange that has installed a wallet offline or a separate wallet management service for each user.

It is desirable to use a wallet and to take measures to reduce the risks of hacking. Wallets are discussed later in this section.

The next section takes a look at the process of mining that supports cryptocurrency trading.

WHAT IS CRYPTOCURRENCY MINING?

Mining refers to the verification procedures for cryptocurrency trading.

Complicated calculations are used to verify transactions for various forms of cryptocurrencies and added to the blockchain. Mining refers to this highly competitive process, which is also called a verification race. Anyone can take part in the mining, and these people are called miners.

Why is this called mining? While the details are not known, it is believed that bitcoins were seen as gold, which created an image of digging for gold in a mine.

Cryptocurrencies are supported by technology called blockchains, which is a distributed ledger or a decentralized network. While further details are given in Chapter 2, at this point it is helpful to know that these are frameworks for keeping records of cryptocurrency transactions. Records are kept of everything from the moment that a cryptocurrency is newly issued to the latest transactions. These records take the form of ledgers, where transactions for every ten minutes are added to the end of the chain. The ledger, or the blocks, are connected as a chain in chronological order; thus, they are called blockchains.

The process of verifying transactions means the verification of new blocks that are added to these blockchains. The process flow for a transaction to be added to a ledger can be described as follows:

Imagine that person A is sending 1 BTC to person B:

1. A creates transaction data to show that A is sending 1 BTC to B's wallet.
2. A encrypts that transfer in a private key that is known only to A. Then A sends the transfer to the distribution network (a network connected to miners throughout the world) along with a public key calculated from the private key. The process up to here is what is called a transfer request.
3. Miners conduct verification to confirm whether the transaction to send money has really been initiated by A.
4. Once the verification is completed, the procedure begins to connect the new block, the ledger for transactions, to the blockchain. Only participants who have succeeded in the verification can connect new blocks to the blockchain.
5. When the new transaction has been added to the block, the 1 BTC sent by A will be received in B's wallet.

Verification is a process of solving extremely difficult mathematical problems, and it is necessary to try values at random to find the values the meet the criteria. For that reason, the system is such that the first miner to find those values is rewarded with cryptocurrency.

An ultra-high-performing computer is required for mining. Dedicated machines for mining have been developed, and there are increasing numbers of facilities that are called mining factories. Many high-performance computers are aligned at mining factories, where verification work is underway.

WHAT ARE WALLETS?

A wallet is like a bank account for storing and managing your cryptocurrency. You have an address that would equate to an account number and a private key that would equate to a personal identification number code.

There are four types of wallets, as follows:

1. Desktop wallets (also called software wallets) – These types of wallets are used by downloading software on your desktop for use in a local environment or offline. Desktop wallets are further broken down into the following two types:
   - A complete type (full-node), e.g. Bitcoin Core – This is the type of wallet where all cryptocurrency blockchains are downloaded and all transaction histories are referenced. A disadvantage is that it will be a load on your PC.
   - A simple type, e.g. Copay, Airbitz, Breadwallet – This type only has the minimum histories required for transactions. It may be said to be specifically for the purpose of storage and sending currency.

   As neither of these are online, there are low risks of hacking; however, risks do exist, such as malfunctions of your PC or theft.

2. Online wallets (also called web wallets) – As you can tell by the name, these are wallets that exist on the internet and may only be used while you're online. There are two types of wallets:
   - Exchange wallets, wallets for transactions – for buying and selling and storage, e.g. a wallet with an exchange
   - Wallets for individual use, e.g. BlockChain.info, Coinbase

Individuals who are new to cryptocurrency investment often leave their newly purchased cryptocurrency in the account that they have opened at an exchange. The status of this cryptocurrency can be said to be that it is stored in an exchange wallet.

What you need to be careful about here is that you cannot tell how an exchange wallet is being managed. From the perspective of the user, it would appear that since he or she has created a personal account, the exchange would create an individual wallet and manage the cryptocurrency for each user; in reality, the exchange may possibly manage the cryptocurrency of all users together. In this case, it could very well lead to all the cryptocurrency being stolen if the exchange were to be hit by a hacking attack.

It is extremely dangerous to store your cryptocurrency in the exchange wallet alone. Thus, the need arises to transfer it to an individual's wallet or to take another such action. Compared with a desktop wallet, an exchange wallet has no risks of a PC malfunction or theft, but needless to say, there are risks of a hacking attack on the exchange or the company that operates the exchange, or bankruptcy.

3. Hardware wallet, e.g. TREZOR, Ledger – This is a method of storing your private keys on a USB or other such device. In order to be able to send or receive cryptocurrency, it is necessary to match the public keys[21] for the cryptocurrency with the private keys.[22] Hardware wallets store these private keys offline. Thus, the cryptocurrency itself is not stored in a hardware wallet.

As hardware wallets are offline, there is little risk of hacking, and the security is strong. Also, you can restore a hardware wallet despite a failure or loss as long as you have your passphrase.

Development is also underway for loading blockchains on smartphones and other such devices. For example, Sirin Labs in Israel unveiled its smartphone FINNEY in 2018, which leverages blockchain technology. It uses a unique operating software (OS) equipped with blockchain features. Because the smartphone itself is a hardware wallet, the security level is high and it enables users to process payments in an efficient manner.

4. Paper wallets – These are methods of storage by printing your private keys and your address on paper. With these wallets, there are no risks of hacking, etc., but there are risks of losing the printed paper or having it stolen. Because of that, services are being developed to store paper wallets in locations like safe deposit boxes at banks.

CAN CRYPTOCURRENCY BE TRUSTED?

You can trust blockchain technology in itself; the technical details are discussed in the next chapter.

It's possible to declare that cryptocurrency for which reliability and safety have been secured through blockchain is dependable from a technical aspect. Particularly in the trading of currencies, duplicate payments cannot take place, but even a single error in a number or a digit can lead to an error. Blockchains provide mutual monitoring between participants in a decentralized network to prevent such incidents from happening.

Because of numerous news reports on hacking incidents, some people have the misconception that cryptocurrency is not safe. But blockchains of cryptocurrencies in themselves have never once been hacked. Whether you look at the Mt. Gox incident or the loss of NEM coins at Coincheck, these were cases where the vulnerability of the exchange systems was targeted.

But note that while blockchain technology may be trusted, that is not to say that all cryptocurrency may be trusted. As mentioned earlier, most of the risks concerning cryptocurrency are due to human factors. Among risks are those relating to several cryptocurrencies that make ICOs and take other such steps through sales talk that is similar to scams.

To repeat, it is most important to develop a critical eye for choosing a good cryptocurrency. And in discerning where to invest, the reliability of the issuing party is an extremely important point that cannot be overlooked. Many of these parties are companies, and companies are people. Depending on the judgments of the managers, companies may succeed and they may fail. The majority of successes and failures are due to human factors.

For example, if you were a major investor who owned 20% of the issues of a cryptocurrency, the value of that cryptocurrency would drop significantly if you sold all 20% at once, which the issuing party would certainly not want. Thus, imagine that the issuing party made a restriction on the amount that a major investor could buy or sell. In such a case, you would only be able to sell a little at a time. If you were to sell with a carte blanche order,[23] you would end up lowering the selling price yourself.

While the issuing party placing restrictions on buying and selling is not an act to directly manipulate prices, it is unfair to prevent the user from conducting transactions as desired. How would you feel if the party that issues your cryptocurrency imposed restrictions on your trading activities? For some cryptocurrencies, the issuing party does impose restrictions on buying and selling.

At the origin of cryptocurrencies was the belief that transactions of money should be more liberal, an ultimate liberalism that aimed for currency to exist beyond the control of states and others in the position of authority or otherwise – thoughts that were mostly anarchist. It was certainly because cryptocurrency appeared to liberally open up areas that were beyond the reach of state powers that cryptocurrency initially took a great leap forward. Many of the people who took part in these moves in the early days became involved in cryptocurrency simply because it was interesting.

When considering that, perhaps it is not possible to escape the charge of being overly idealist, but the position to make profit, even if it means hindering the natural moves of the market, is not something that can be acknowledged.

The next chapter takes a close look at the history and technical aspect of the framework of blockchains.

CHAPTER 2

BLOCKCHAINS THAT SUPPORT CRYPTOCURRENCY

WHO DEVELOPED CRYPTOCURRENCY AND HOW?

The origin of cryptocurrency can be traced back to a paper released by Satoshi Nakamoto in 2008. This paper, "Bitcoin: A Peer-to-Peer Electronic Cash System",[1] is available online.

This paper is said to have described a ground-breaking invention. It is structured as follows:

1. Introduction
2. (Electronic currency) transactions
3. Timestamp server
4. Proof-of-work (proof of the volume of calculations)
5. Network
6. Incentive (for network participants)
7. Reclaiming disk space
8. Simplified payment verification
9. Combining and splitting value (of electronic currency)
10. Privacy
11. Calculations (mathematic basis)
12. Conclusion

An outline of Nakamoto's paper is as follows:

- By using a framework of a peer-to-peer (P2P) network that connects terminals without establishing a central server, it is possible to conduct direct trade for electronic currency.
- An electronic signature system is effective to a certain extent; however, in order to avoid duplicate payments (double spending), it may not be called complete so long as monitoring by a third party is required.
- The connections of transaction history (chain) itself is defined as electronic currency (this will be explained in detail later).
- By disclosing all transactions on the network and having network participants approve them, copying and altering transaction information will be extremely difficult technologically and not worth the cost.
- System security will be maintained if the aggregate CPU power held by participants with goodwill who are connected on the network far exceeds the CPU of those who want to commit fraud.
- By building a system that is not mediated by a third party, or a system that does not rely on trust, it will be possible to conduct safe transactions of electronic currency at low costs.

Roles are established for legal currencies; for example, "it is issued by a central bank" or "transactions are monitored by a bank or financial institution, or a trusted third party".

In the case of bitcoin, however, rather than disclosing transaction history on the network, it turned all of its participants into administrators. Instead of having monitoring by a "trusted third party", this is achieved by an overwhelmingly large number of network participants.

The safety of bitcoin transactions is supported by building a system in which the majority of participants will determine it to be more to their profit to conduct 'transaction approval', an act of goodwill, rather than conduct wrongdoing. In other words, it is the participants who do both the issuing and who monitor transactions. The basis of thought for cryptocurrency is to have participants mutually recognize value, conduct reciprocal monitoring against wrongdoing and build value.

Also, transaction costs are lowered if transactions can be conducted safely without being monitored or controlled by a trusted third party, such as a financial institution like a bank or credit information institution. Then the transactions become a casual, everyday occurrence. The Nakamoto paper also touches on this point at the outset.

THE HISTORY OF BITCOIN

CHRONOLOGICAL TIMELINE FOR BITCOIN

Major events and total volume issued (ratio versus maximum limit for issues)/value)

2008

October – Satoshi Nakamoto's paper is released

Total amount issued: 0 (0%)

Value: 0 USD

2009

January – The birth of bitcoin

Total amount issued: 2,625,000 (12.5%)

Value: 0.0009 USD

(As of 3 January)

2010

February – The Bitcoin Market, the world's first online cryptocurrency exchange for exchanging bitcoins with the US dollar, is opened in the USA

Total amount issued: 5,250,000 (25%)

Value: 0.08 USD
(As of 22 April)

2011

March – The exchange BritCoin is established in Britain; the exchange Bitcoin Brasil is opened in Brazil

Total amount issued: 10,500,000 (50%)

Value: 3.19 USD
(As of 14 December)

2012

Negative information stands out; however, value recovers

Total amount issued: 11,812,500 (56.25%)

Value: 12.16 USD
(As of 28 November)

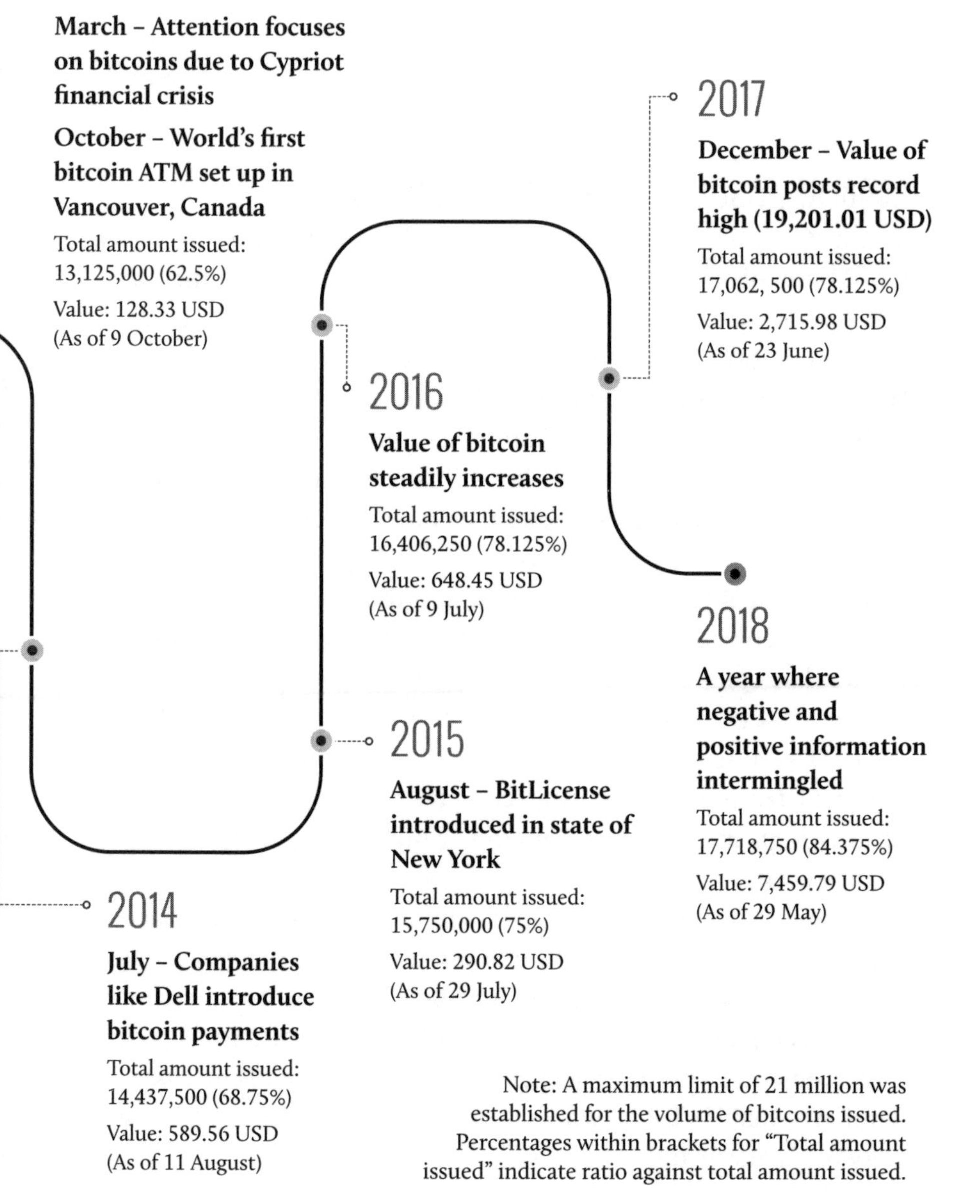

Note: A maximum limit of 21 million was established for the volume of bitcoins issued. Percentages within brackets for "Total amount issued" indicate ratio against total amount issued.

References: bitcoin.com, historyofbitcoin.org, bitcoinwiki

As many people know, bitcoins are a presence that symbolize cryptocurrency. To know the history of bitcoin is to know the history of cryptocurrency.

An introduction to the history of bitcoin follows, based on the volume of bitcoins issued, its price fluctuations and major events.

2008: RELEASE OF SATOSHI NAKAMOTO'S PAPER

The history of cryptocurrency begins with the birth of bitcoin. On 31 October 2008, Satoshi Nakamoto released a paper, as noted above, on the electronic currency bitcoin on a cryptography (encryption technology) mailing list. Bitcoin was not born from an academic paper but instead from a paper on the internet.

Nothing about Satoshi Nakamoto is known – whether Nakamoto is a male or female, an individual or a group, a Japanese national or a Japanese-American. While the person's identity remains a mystery, Nakamoto is known widely as the person who contrived the Bitcoin protocol and Bitcoin Core/Bitcoin-Qt.

The Bitcoin protocol refers to the procedures and arrangements that computers should follow. For example, the protocol decides that the size of one block in a blockchain shall be 1 MB. While it is possible to change the protocol if agreement can be obtained from a number that exceeds a certain number, that ratio is high in the case of bitcoin, which makes it difficult to change easily.

Bitcoin Core refers to an open source program for conducting bitcoin transactions and for mining. Anyone can download and use this program from GitHub (https://github.com), a software development platform. It is possible for anyone to suggest improvements; whether a suggestion will be adopted is discussed within the mailing list, in which people associated with the Bitcoin Network[2] participate.

2009: THE BIRTH OF BITCOIN

After the paper was unveiled, in 2009 Satoshi Nakamoto released the first edition of Bitcoin Core (version 0.1). Along with that, operations for bitcoin began. It became possible for anyone to participate in the bitcoin network.

Programmers throughout the world who agreed with Satoshi Nakamoto's paper made improvements to version 0.1, and thus bitcoin was born. It is said that it was improved by more than 90%. The first block in bitcoin's blockchain is the genesis block, which was created by Satoshi Nakamoto on 3 January 2009. Satoshi Nakamoto was the first owner of bitcoins in the world.

The world's first bitcoin transaction took place the following year: on 12 January 2010, 50 BTC were sent (transferred) from Satoshi Nakamoto to Hal Finney, a programmer and expert on encryption. Finney, one of the first individuals to take an interest in Satoshi Nakamoto's paper, received on a cryptography mailing list,[3] became the first bitcoin holder.

On 5 October 2010, an exchange rate between bitcoins and legal currency was indicated for the first time by New Liberty Standard (an individual with this nickname on bitcoin forum). The price at the time was 1,309.03 BTC to the dollar. The rate was calculated from the electricity charge needed for mining bitcoin.

The first transaction was held on 12 October 2010 between bitcoins and legal currency: New Liberty Standard bought 5,050 BTC for 5.02 USD. The rate had fallen 23.16% from the price calculated based on electricity charges needed for mining.

Between 2008, when Satoshi Nakamoto's paper was released, and the following year, very few people in the world knew about bitcoin. You could say that it was the preserve of some IT nerds.

2010: THE WORLD'S FIRST BITCOIN PAYMENT

The Bitcoin Market, an online cryptocurrency exchange for exchanging bitcoins with the US dollar, was set up in the USA in February 2010, making it possible to buy and sell bitcoins. The first transaction on the Bitcoin Market was 1 BTC at 8 cents.

The price indicated when New Liberty Standard conducted a transaction between bitcoins and legal currency on 5 October 2009 was 1,309.03 BTC to 1 USD (1 BTC at 0.0763 cents). This is an increase of approximately 104.8 times in nearly four months.

On 22 May the following year, the first bitcoin settlement was completed in Florida. On 18 May 2010, an engineer named Laszlo Hanyecz made a post on a bulletin board called Bitcoin Forum,[4] a venue for holding discussions on cryptocurrency, saying that he wanted to use bitcoins to buy a pizza; the transaction was completed four days later. This famous story is known as bitcoin pizza day.

At that time, Hanyecz obtained two pizzas priced at approximately 25 USD for 10,000 BTC. But it wasn't as if the pizza shop approved of the value of bitcoins. It was simply that another person received Hanyecz's bitcoins and bought the pizzas on his behalf.

At the time, bitcoins were in a sense like a game currency for IT nerds. But it is possible to say that the payments for these two pizzas suggested various possibilities for bitcoins.

On 11 July of the same year, bitcoins were featured on Slashdot, an electronic bulletin board in the USA that chiefly picks up computer news, which led to people other than some IT nerds finding out about the existence of bitcoins.

And on July 18, Jed McCaleb, a programmer who read the Slashdot article, opened a bitcoin exchange and called it Mt. Gox. This exchange restored the domain name of an online exchange for buying and selling trading cards that was launched in 2007, immediately closed and remained in a dormant state.[5]

On the other hand, the vulnerability of bitcoin was pointed out on 15 August when 194 billion BTC were forged. This is described as the worst security incident in the history of bitcoin, but the situation was corrected by a volunteer development team, leaving barely any impact. (The safety of bitcoin will be discussed later.)

2011: THE BITCOIN BUBBLE

Bitcoin transactions became active in 2011. In February of the same year, the price of 1 BTC soared as high as 1 USD. Compared with the initial rate at which bitcoin was traded on the Bitcoin Market, at 8 cents to 1 BTC, the rate rose 12.5 times.

In March 2011, Jed McCaleb sold Mt. Gox to Tibanne Co. Ltd.,[6] a web hosting company operated by Mark Karpelès, a French programmer who lives in Tokyo. This made Mt. Gox the first bitcoin exchange operated by a company whose head office is registered in Japan (it later grew to become the world's biggest bitcoin exchange in 2013). No particular licences were required, as licences such as Japan's Financial Services Agency's licence for virtual currency exchange service providers did not exist until 2011.

It was during the same month, March 2011, that BritCoin, Britain's first bitcoin exchange, was opened. The name was later changed to Intersango, but the exchange closed in 2012.

In March 2011, Bitcoin Brasil opened in Brazil.

In April 2013, Bitmarket.eu, a currency exchange, was opened, and it became possible to conduct transactions between bitcoin and multiple legal currencies, including the euro and the zloty (Poland's currency). Unfortunately, this exchange was closed at the end of October 2013 due to reasons that included financial difficulties.

It was also during this month that the *Economist* in the UK printed a feature on bitcoins as "true digital cash". However, bitcoin also gained attention for bad reasons too. Bitcoin was picked up by the major media for having been used in drug trafficking payments on a black-market website called Silk Road, which was closed by the FBI in October 2013.

The fact that bitcoin was used for criminal activity on a black-market site is bad for the reputation of cryptocurrency, but it is also proof of demand for bitcoin transactions and boosted the value of bitcoins as an object to invest in.

On 19 June 2013, Mt. Gox was hit by a hacking attack. In this incident, user information and passwords were stolen and transactions were suspended for about a week. Hacking incidents also occurred at other exchanges, and the price of bitcoins dropped by 80%, from 12 USD to 1 BTC to as low as 2 USD. After that, increases in the value of bitcoins were sluggish, with the value at around 5 USD until the middle of 2012.

2012: THE VALUE OF BITCOIN RECOVERS

In 2012, the value of bitcoins fell further, due in part to the impact of the Mt. Gox incident that occurred the previous year. There were, however, significant increases in opportunities for people to discover bitcoin, including through negative news. As a result, the awareness level of bitcoins increased worldwide during 2012.

On the other hand, there was a leak of internal information at the FBI that said that "chances were high that bitcoin would be used for illegal acts" (compiled on 26 April).[7] The material suggested that "the cryptocurrency bitcoin: several of its characteristics will clearly become obstacles in preventing illegal acts" and included the following:

- "Bitcoin is a virtual currency that has decentralized peer-to-peer networks as its foundation. It has the potential to become a method for creating, moving, laundering assets with a certain level of anonymity or for stealing illegal assets."
- "Cyber criminals are likely to us bitcoins in addition to other existing virtual currencies as a method of payment in the near future. The FBI evaluates medium-level probability of this."
- "When bitcoin becomes stable and achieves a high level of recognition, it is likely to be used as a more convenient tool

> in various types of illegal activities. And this does not stop in the area of cybercrime. Bitcoin is not under a centralized authority. For that reason, it will be difficult for judiciary authorities to find suspicious activities, identify the users and extract transaction records. This is the point that will attract criminals."

Automattic Inc., which operates the open-source software WordPress, introduced bitcoin settlements on 15 November 2012, which made it the biggest business to accept bitcoin payments.

2013: BITCOIN ATTRACTS ATTENTION

The Cypriot financial crisis that occurred in March 2013 brought attention to bitcoin and prompted funds to flow into bitcoin, chiefly in the EU region. This was because cryptocurrency, which is not controlled by governments or financial institutions, is not impacted by the freezing of accounts. The crisis pushed up the market capitalization of bitcoin to exceed 1 billion USD, and at one point it soared as high as 266 USD to 1 BTC. This made it 3,325 times higher than its value of 8 cents in 2010.

The Cypriot financial crisis arose when Greek government bonds, owned by Greek banks, which had close ties with Cyprus, turned into massive bad debts due to the financial crisis in Greece in 2010.

The EU agreed to provide Cyprus with financial support on the condition that the government of Cyprus would implement a strict financial policy that would result in the closing of accounts and restrictions being imposed on bank withdrawals.

The policy turned out to be a maximum of 9.9% taxes on all accounts held by Cypriot citizens. Account holders rushed to banks and financial institutions, but a situation occurred where they could not withdraw money. Their sense of distrust in their government, banks and financial institutions led to an increasing number of citizens buying bitcoins to protect their assets.

This made the price of bitcoins soar, and bitcoins gained global attention as an independent currency that was not mediated by governments or banks (central authorities). Furthermore, the focus that bitcoin gained among investors and speculative investors as an object for investment continued to push up the price of bitcoins.

Amid such moves, the world again found other potential for bitcoins. In October 2013, the world's first bitcoin ATM was set up in Vancouver, Canada. At a bitcoin ATM, you can buy bitcoins by depositing cash.

After this, wealthy Chinese nationals began to buy up bitcoins.

On 17 November, 503.10 USD was posted on Mt. Gox. On 20 November, trading volume at BTC China, a bitcoin exchange in China, became double that at Mt. Gox, and therefore made it the biggest exchange in the world.

As a result, the value of bitcoin soared to 1,200 USD to 1 BTC and bitcoin's market capitalization exceeded 10 billion USD. Concerned by such a situation, the Chinese authorities announced in December 2013 that they would forbid Chinese financial institutions from conducting bitcoin transactions as businesses. News reports on the announcement caused a drop in the price of bitcoin to as low as 700 USD to 1 BTC.

Furthermore, on 4 December, NHK television (NIPPON HOSO KYOKAI, or Japan Broadcasting Corporation) televised a feature on bitcoins on one of its programmes in Japan. The broadcast prompted many Japanese to learn about bitcoins.

2014: INTRODUCTION OF BITCOIN PAYMENTS

In 2014, various companies throughout the world announced that they would accept bitcoin payments.

Overstock.com, a major US online retailer, began accepting bitcoin payments in January 2014.

On 7 February, a hacking incident occurred where more than 11.4 billion yen in bitcoins was stolen from a bitcoin exchange operated by Mt. Gox. Bitcoin transactions at Mt. Gox were suspended two days later. A week after the incident, the value of bitcoins plummeted approximately 50%, from 717 USD to 1 BTC to 400 USD.

Inaccurate reports in Japan, where the head office of Mt. Gox was located, suggested that companies had gone bankrupt because of the drop in the value of bitcoins following reports of this incident. This created a negative impression among the Japanese people with regard to bitcoins and cryptocurrency.

In April 2014, etwings, the world's first Monacoin exchange, was born. Monacoins were Japan's first domestic cryptocurrency, released in January 2014. (Cryptocurrencies other than bitcoins are collectively referred to as altcoins, as explained later in the book.) Etwings was acquired by another cryptocurrency exchange called Zaif in 2015. Incidentally, Zaif became the first exchange to conduct transactions between the Japanese yen and cryptocurrencies and between other cryptocurrencies in Japan.

On 26 May, bitFlyer, established in January 2014, began services as an exchange and became the biggest cryptocurrency exchange in Japan.

In June 2014, the major online travel agency Expedia began accepting bitcoin payments for hotel bookings.

Also, Japan's first bitcoin ATM was set up in Tokyo. Bitcoin Japan, a company that we (Joe McKenzie) and Roger Ver had been involved in, set up this bitcoin ATM. The company later changed its name and presently continues to exist as a different company with the same name, Bitcoin Japan.

On 17 July 2014, the New York Department of Financial Services announced its proposal for BitLicense,[8] a licensing system for businesses associated with bitcoin, for preventing the use of bitcoins for illegal activities.

On 18 July 2014, the multinational computer technology company Dell began introducing bitcoin settlements within the USA. In September, PayPal announced that it would begin dealing with bitcoin settlements. And on 11 December, the Microsoft Corporation began accepting requests for bitcoin payments, although this was limited to people residing in the USA.

While the handling of bitcoin transactions by financial institutions was prohibited in China, the restriction could not be imposed on transactions between individuals, and Chinese citizens engaged actively in trading.

Although transaction prices fluctuated significantly throughout the year, there was a lack of factors to push up the price as the year saw a drop from 700 USD to 300 USD to 1 BTC.

2015: ANNOUNCEMENT OF BITLICENSE

In 2015, BitLicense came into force in the state of New York.

On 4 January 2015, a hacking incident occurred at Bitstamp, a bitcoin exchange based in Luxembourg. It announced that 5.3 million USD (at the time) in bitcoin had been stolen.

On 1 August 2015, Mark Karpelès of Mt. Gox was suspected of falsifying data in his account to increase its balance. Karpelès was arrested in Japan on 21 August by the National Police Agency on suspicion of the illegal production and use of private electromagnetic records and indicted on charges of corporate embezzlement for embezzling money from his customers.

On 8 August 2015, the New York State Department of Financial Services took a step ahead of the world to introduce BitLicense, a licensing system for operators associated with bitcoin. This made it necessary for bitcoin-related businesses in the state of New York to obtain a licence. As stated earlier, the examinations are extremely tough and complicated, and the licensing system led many cryptocurrency-related businesses to leave the state of New York. Bitcoin users, however, could feel confident that good businesses had been selected, which boosted their sense of security with regard to cryptocurrency trading.

On 15 August 2015, the bitcoin community became divided due to a scalability issue (the problem of the speed of data processing slowing down and transactions taking time when large volumes of transactions take place at once). Mike Hearn and Gavin Andresen, software developers who had been conducting integral developments in bitcoin, released Bitcoin XT.

In October 2015, the European Court of Justice (ECJ) handed down a decision that bitcoin transactions will be exempt from value-added tax (VAT).[9] As bitcoin transactions in Europe would not be subject to taxes, bitcoin's value rose as high as 400 USD to 1 BTC. On 31 October, bitcoin was used on the cover of the British magazine *The Economist*.[10] The article focused on the usability of blockchain technology at banks and government institutions.

On 2 December 2015, Bitcoin Unlimited was released, following the release of Bitcoin XT Coins, derived from bitcoin (see "Coins derived from bitcoin" in Chapter 3).

2016: INCREASE IN THE VALUE OF BITCOIN

During 2016, the value of bitcoin steadily increased.

Software developer Mike Hearn departed from the development of bitcoin due to the scalability issue the previous year, in 2015. Mike Hearn had led the technical team at Google. Hearn commented in his blog that "Bitcoin has failed",[11] and his departure triggered the value of bitcoin to fall to around 50 USD.

On 10 February 2016, Bitcoin Classic was released, to follow the releases of Bitcoin XT and Bitcoin Unlimited.

On 21 February 2016, noteworthy members of the bitcoin community held a conference in Hong Kong on development plans for expanding bitcoin. At this conference, a public statement was made that an agreement had been reached to create a hard fork for the bitcoin protocol to increase the limited block size from 2 to 4 megabytes (MB) by July 2016. Hard fork means an update or change in the software for determining how a blockchain is used. This would cause a division in the blockchain; the details on this will be touched on later.

On 1 March 2016, bitcoin payments became possible at a Japan-based electronic commerce and internet company, DMM.com. It became the first big company in Japan to incorporate bitcoin settlements.

On 27 April 2016, bitcoin payments also began at Steam, a platform for downloads and sales of PC games in the USA.

On 2 August 2016, Bitfinex, an exchange in Hong Kong, was hit by a hacking attack, and approximately 120,000 BTC (approximately 72 million USD), the largest amount in history, was stolen. An announcement was made in 2017 that repayments to customers who had suffered damage had been completed.

At the end of 2016, the impact of India's ban on the use of large banknotes and the 500% inflation in Venezuela made bitcoin soar to 10,000 USD to 1 BTC.

2017: BITCOIN VALUE SOARS TO RECORD LEVELS

In 2017, the value of bitcoin soared to record levels.

On 9 February 2017, OKCoin, BTCC and Huobi, major cryptocurrency exchanges in China, were closed after bitcoin was said to have been used for money laundering.

On 1 April 2017, an amended Payment Services Act came into force in Japan.[12] According to this law, cryptocurrency (the term virtual currency is used under the law) was exempt from consumption tax. The term virtual currency exchange service was also defined, and it became necessary for virtual currency exchange service providers to register. It was in this way that bitcoin transactions came under the supervision of the Financial Services Agency.

On 1 August 2017, Bitcoin Cash was born to resolve the issue of scalability by increasing the volume of blocks themselves within blockchains.

Discussions have been held around the world on updating the methods for sending bitcoins and for improving the speed of processing.

While there had been concerns over decline in the value due to the divisions created by updating in bitcoins in order to further breakdowns, there was not as much impact on value as anticipated when Bitcoin Cash came to be. It also came under the spotlight that cryptocurrency exchanges distributed an equal amount of Bitcoin Cash to users who were in possession of bitcoins, free of charge.

On 4 September 2017, the Chinese government announced that it would impose a complete ban on ICOs in China. ICOs refer to the procurement of funds/crowdfunding from the issue of coins (digital tokens/cryptocurrency). The Chinese government made the procurement of funds through ICOs illegal and subject to punishment.

On 18 December 2017, the value of bitcoin exceeded 18,000 USD to 1 BTC – a record high. The cause of this was that the Chicago Mercantile Exchange (CME), the world's biggest market for futures trading, began trading bitcoin futures. In November of the same year, the Chicago Board Options Exchange (Cboe), a major US market for futures trading, had also begun bitcoin futures trading.

2018: AN ENTANGLEMENT OF VARIOUS TYPES OF INFORMATION

During 2018, both negative and positive information were entangled.

On 26 January 2018, a hacking incident occurred at Japanese exchange Coincheck, where the equivalent of about 5.8 million yen of the cryptocurrency NEM had been stolen. After this incident, Japan's Financial Services Agency began to conduct site inspections at virtual currency exchange service providers and quasi operators and started to issue orders for business improvement and orders to suspend business.[13]

This served to cool down investor sentiment in Japan, and the value of many cryptocurrencies fell. Although exchanges had seen a rush of individual investors who wanted to open accounts the previous year, self-restraint was practised, also on advertising activities such as television commercials.

Cryptocurrency was, for the first time, included in the agenda of the G20 meeting, a meeting of finance ministers and central bank governors from 20 countries, held in March 2018. Cryptocurrency was described as an encrypted asset that lacked the characteristics of a legal currency. In conclusion, an appeal was made for cryptocurrency's monitoring by an international institution in order to deal with problems such as money laundering and the use of cryptocurrency for terrorist financing. A permit and licensing system was introduced for virtual currency exchange service providers, and an agreement was reached on an objective to establish regulations.[14] The same details were confirmed at a G20 held in July 2018.

In the USA, a decision was handed down by the US District Court in March 2018 that cryptocurrencies in the form of bitcoins should be subject to regulations imposed by the US Commodity Futures Trading Commission (CFTC).[15] The chair of the US Securities and Exchange Commission (SEC) also indicated his opinion that ICO tokens would be subject to SEC regulations as securities.

There were also many positive moves concerning cryptocurrency, such as back-to-back news on senior management at famous financial institutions making career changes to cryptocurrency start-ups.[16]

In June 2018, PricewaterhouseCoopers (PwC), one of the four major accounting firms in the world, together with cooperation from Switzerland's Crypto Valley Association, released a report that 537 ICOs were initiated between January and May of 2018 and that the amount of funds procured had exceeded 1.37 billion USD.[17] In fact, there were 552 cases in 2017 with procured amounts exceeding 7 billion USD, which indicated that the ICO boom was still underway.[18]

In July 2018, the LINE Corporation, a Tokyo-based subsidiary of the South Korean internet search giant Naver Corporation, opened a cryptocurrency exchange called BITBOX. It only deals with transactions between cryptocurrencies and offers services worldwide, with the exception of Japan and the USA.

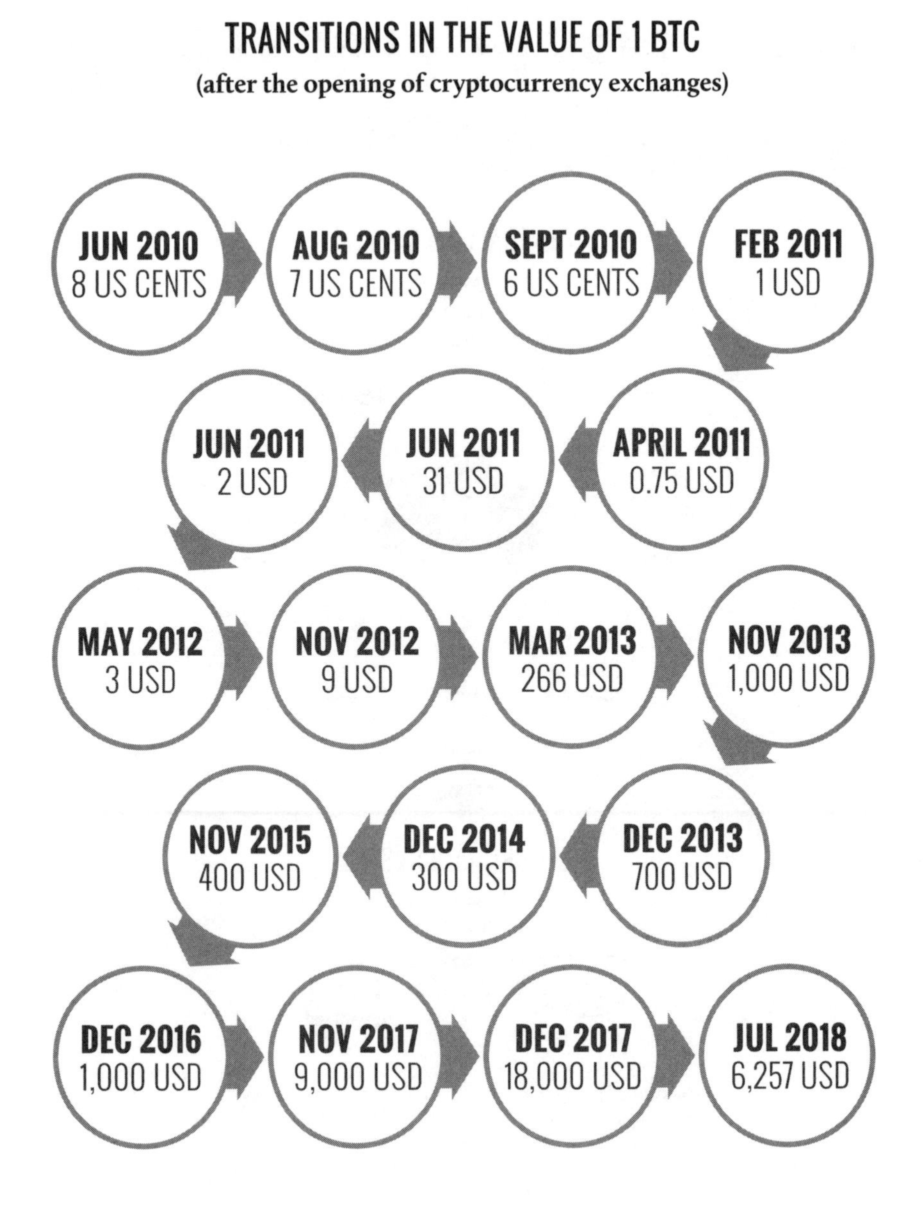
TRANSITIONS IN THE VALUE OF 1 BTC
(after the opening of cryptocurrency exchanges)
JUN 2010
8 US CENTS
AUG 2010
7 US CENTS
SEPT 2010
6 US CENTS
FEB 2011
1 USD
APRIL 2011
0.75 USD
JUN 2011
31 USD
JUN 2011
2 USD
MAY 2012
3 USD
NOV 2012
9 USD
MAR 2013
266 USD
NOV 2013
1,000 USD
DEC 2013
700 USD
DEC 2014
300 USD
NOV 2015
400 USD
DEC 2016
1,000 USD
NOV 2017
9,000 USD
DEC 2017
18,000 USD
JUL 2018
6,257 USD

WHAT TYPE OF BLOCKCHAIN SUPPORTS BITCOIN?

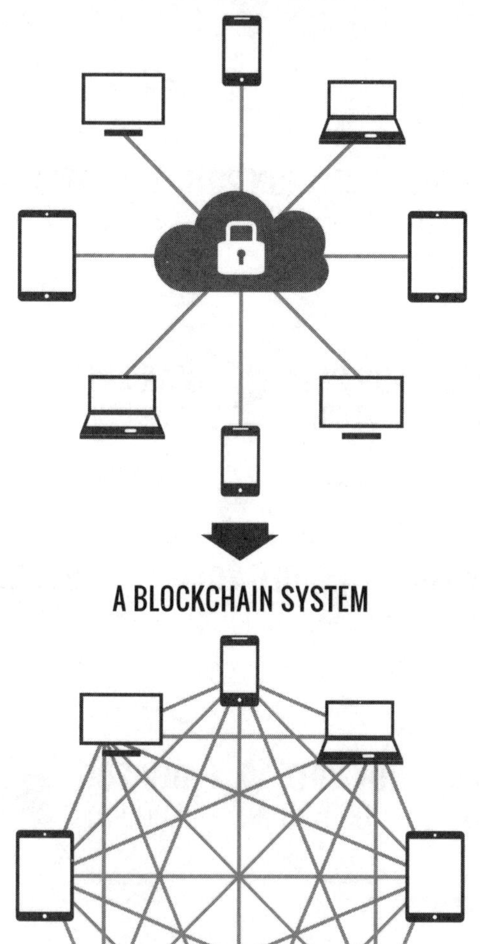

As mentioned before, bitcoins are supported by technology called blockchains. The idea for a digital currency (bitcoin) that enables trading and transfer at low costs without the need for mediation by a third party such as a bank or financial institution was made possible by blockchains. Blockchains were contrived by Satoshi Nakamoto, and improvements to them were made by software developers throughout the world.

Essentially a blockchain is a framework so that transaction records cannot be rewritten. Wrongful acts such as using bitcoins that have already been used once or using fake bitcoins to make a payment are not possible if transaction records cannot be rewritten.

This characteristics of a blockchain can be summarized as:

- It is established as a P2P network
- Information on transactions is disclosed
- Anyone can take part in the network

The P2P characteristics of a blockchain refer to a system where parties exchange data on terminals that are connected on the network. In other words, there are no fixed positions like a server that stores and provides data or clients who request access to that data.

The lack of a central server also means that, for example, the system (server) at a financial institution such as a bank will not mediate. The lack of a specific party in authority makes it possible to realize transactions at low costs.

Also, individual computers that are connected to the P2P network will bring together storage space for data and processing capacity. For that reason, a suspension in the server will not suspend the entire system or incur a loss of data. The system is therefore supported by all participants; the blockchain will never break down, even when a single computer breaks down.

Disclosure of information on transactions, which is the second characteristic mentioned, literally refers to the disclosure of all past transaction details on the network. It is necessary for information on transactions to be disclosed and for individual transactions to be approved by a large number of participants on the network. For that reason, it is extremely difficult to alter transaction records, making it possible to prevent forgery and duplicate use without the need to have a controlling entity.

In the bitcoin blockchain, a new block is made every ten minutes with records of transactions that have taken place, which are connected in chronological order. An individual code is allocated to each of these blocks. Unless consistency is established between these codes, a new block will not be added to the chain. This process equates to verification.

Enormous volumes of calculations are required to establish consistency between the codes (the verification process), and they must be approved by a majority of the computer calculation volume. Thus it isn't easy to tamper with the blocks or to shuffle the order of these blocks.

One programmer explained that "a blockchain is like continuing to put Blu-ray discs in a bucket and then firming it with cement". In order to rewrite data recorded on discs, you need to break down the cement and then extract a disc at a time ... the work incurred would be mind-boggling. In other words, while it may not be possible to say that rewriting and fabrication are entirely impossible, they would be extremely difficult.

The third characteristic of a blockchain – that is is a network in which anyone can take part – is indeed the very point in Satoshi Nakamoto's paper that was groundbreaking. This is because the transaction ledger for bitcoin, or its blockchain, was made into something that everyone can mutually manage and use rather than something that belonged to a specific administrator or party of authority.

For example, a bank passbook may usually only be seen by the bank and the account holder, whereas the transaction histories in blockchains are accessible to everyone taking part in the network, so anyone can see records of transactions being conducted; however, they can't see the details, since these are encrypted, thus protecting privacy. The spirit of freedom and equality are expressed in blockchains.

HOW DO BLOCKCHAINS FUNCTION?

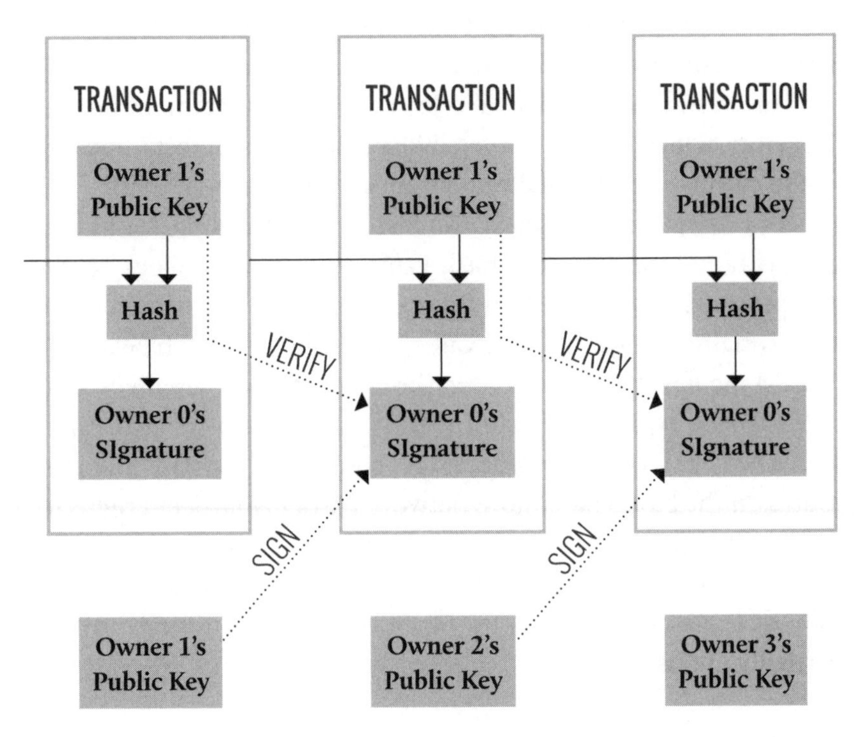

Source: https://bitcoin.org/bitcoin.pdf

Transaction histories in blockchains are linked in a chain and form at an average of a block every ten minutes. Transactions conducted on the cryptocurrency network are stored in data blocks (blocks), which are linked in a chain in chronological order, which is why it is called a blockchain.

A blockchain is supported by technologies like hash values, digital signatures and consensus algorithms.

HASH VALUES

In each block, an encrypted numerical value called a hash value indicating the record of past transaction contents (transaction history), new transaction contents, and the content of the block generated one time ago is stored.

This hash value is calculated by a calculation method called a hash function, but it has irreversibility so that it is almost impossible to calculate an original value from a hash value.

For example, if the transaction history at a certain point in the past is tampered with, the hash value stored in the block to be tampered with is changed. In this case, however, it is necessary to sequentially change the hash values of all the chained blocks following the next block. Moreover, the chain of newly rebuilt blocks needs to be regarded as valid data by the consensus algorithm described later. However, since larger computing capacity concentrates on the blockchain more network participants deem right, it is almost impossible for malicious minorities to get approval at a rate that exceeds that agreement formation. As a result, falsification of transaction records in the blockchain is considered to be virtually impossible.

DIGITAL SIGNATURES

A technology called a digital signature is a function used to prevent identity fraud and manipulation when you send bitcoins. Transaction records, which are encrypted as hash values using a hash function, continue to be passed through digital signature technology using public key cryptography, which is an encryption method that allows separate keys (procedures) for encryption and decryption to be used to expose the key of encryption.

Public key cryptography uses two mathematically related keys – a public key and a private key – for encryption and decryption (decoding an encryption to the original value). The sender uses the public key that the recipient has disclosed to encrypt data, and the recipient uses a private key that only he or she has to decrypt the data. By using digital signatures like this for transactions such as sending money, only the individual who is in possession of the correct cryptocurrency is able to send cryptocurrency in a correct manner.

The term digital signature technology may sound complicated, but the function is the same as signing your name on a paper agreement. There are two points to the function that are referred to here:

- It is proof that the individual has signed his or her name
- It cannot be used for other contracts, therefore is only effective for the agreement that has been signed

CONSENSUS ALGORITHM

A consensus algorithm, also called a building agreement, refers to the algorithm in a blockchain network that establishes rules for adding blocks.

Bitcoin uses an algorithm called Proof of Work (PoW). In bitcoin's PoW, the validity of blocks is approved by all participants an average of every ten minutes to create new blocks.

An enormous amount of calculation processing is needed for this validation work, which checks that there has been no tampering and that no duplicate uses have been made. Mining refers to this process.

Blocks can only be generated in bitcoin's blockchain once every ten minutes on average. This 'on average' part is an extreme nuisance – it may be possible to process a calculation in three minutes, while it may not be possible to complete another calculation in an hour. It isn't possible to precisely predict the speed of processing. Although bitcoin has been considered something of a great invention, various issues have been incurred from the aspect of functionality with the passage of time.

WHAT PROBLEMS EXIST WITH BITCOIN?

A problem that presently exists with bitcoin is scalability. This problem has become evident with the increased volume of bitcoin transactions and refers to the increasing processing speed and costs of processing. While bitcoin had previously been a quick method for sending money, with low handling fees, it has now become a slow and expensive method of transferring funds.

As a block is generated on average every ten minutes, waiting is incurred if many transactions take place simultaneously. Processing speed can slow down because of a sudden increase in bitcoin transactions worldwide.

Blockchains exist as miners who participate in the bitcoin network conduct the verification work. As mentioned previously, miners are compensated for their efforts with bitcoins, which are newly issued, and handling charges paid by users at the time of their transactions.

While the volume of the former, the newly issued bitcoins, is established according to the bitcoin program, the handling charges may be set by users. For this reason, miners give priority to user approvals that are set at higher rates. Therefore, handling charges increase like an auction, because unless handling fees are set at high rates, the status of waiting will continue.

There are said to be cases today, as the volume of transactions has significantly increased, where the handling charge for sending 1 USD in bitcoin was 15 USD, and it took a week for the money to be received. Bitcoin came into being as a free and convenient digital currency, but a fee of 15 USD to transfer 1 USD is far too inconvenient.

HOW CAN THE ISSUES WITH BITCOIN BE RESOLVED?

It has been difficult to find a fundamental solution for the scalability problem of bitcoin by simply improving the bitcoin program. For that reason, individuals have come forward who want to make a better cryptocurrency. The cryptocurrency that was developed is called alternative coin, abbreviated as altcoin. Altcoin has now become a generic term for cryptocurrencies other than bitcoins. For example, Bitcoin Cash, Ripple and Ethereum are also altcoins.

The lack of a designated administrator or people with authority is why the issues of transaction speed and high handling charges could not be resolved for bitcoin. This is a characteristic of bitcoin, and it been both an advantage and a disadvantage.

The advantage is that because everyone who takes part in the network is both an administrator and person of authority, it was possible to exchange opinions freely and equally. It is said that 90% of improvements were made compared with the bitcoin program during the creation period.

The disadvantage is that because there are no designated administrators or people of authority, it isn't possible for someone to take command for making improvements. As the number of network participants increased, it was no longer possible to make smooth improvements in the program.

Due to such challenges with bitcoin, 'centralized cryptocurrencies' like Ripple and 'decentralized cryptocurrencies' like Ethereum came into being.

Chapter 3 will look into the current state of altcoins and cryptocurrencies.

CHAPTER 3

THE PRESENT STATUS OF CRYPTOCURRENCY

WHAT TYPES OF CRYPTOCURRENCIES ARE THERE?

Bitcoin, known broadly as the world's first cryptocurrency, is a decentralized cryptocurrency for which no issuing party exists. While bitcoin is called a key currency[1] for cryptocurrency, the number of participants on its network has increased over time and various issues have arisen, as mentioned earlier.

There are said to be 2,000 or 3,000 types of cryptocurrencies. An introduction is provided here to the three major cryptocurrencies. They are Ripple, Ethereum and Bitcoin Cash.

Bitcoin Cash is a new cryptocurrency that was developed in August 2017. Today, Bitcoin Cash is gaining attention as a new cryptocurrency that resolves the issues faced by bitcoin in delayed transfers and soaring handling fees. Like bitcoin, Bitcoin Cash is a decentralized cryptocurrency and mining is possible.

Ripple is a centralized cryptocurrency and the only blockchain network for international transfers of cash for companies worldwide. Ripple resolved challenges faced by bitcoin such as scalability and the enormous amount of electric power required for mining. With Ripple, it is possible to complete payments and transfers, which take ten minutes on average for bitcoin, in a few seconds, and handling charges are lower. Mining isn't possible, as Ripple is a centralized cryptocurrency.

A characteristic of Ethereum is that it has a smart contract function with the application of blockchain. A smart contract function enables automatic processing of contracts. With automatic processing of contracts, it is possible to execute contracts without a third-party institution, i.e. a mediator.

While transaction records for bitcoins only include details such as "person A will send 10 BTC to person B", the use of a smart contract function enables the recording of the transaction history "person A will send 10 BTC to person B" as well as the contract detail such as "person B will hand over the copyright for his or her song to person A" to be executed automatically.

Also, through the use of its structure, Ethereum is also leveraged as a platform for creating apps. In these ways, Ethereum is a highly versatile program that doesn't stop with uses for cryptocurrency. It is a decentralized cryptocurrency, as is bitcoin, and mining is possible.

COINS DERIVED FROM BITCOIN

	BITCOIN XT	BITCOIN UNLIMITED	BITCOIN CLASSICS	BITCOIN CASH	BITCOIN GOLD
Characteristics:	Eases maximum limits for a single block size	Enlarges sizes of blocks or else compresses Bitcoin Core	Changes quantity of a single block size to 2 MB	Changes quantity of a single block size to 8 MB	Changes mining algorithm (adjusts level of difficulty for each block; maintains time required for generating new blocks at a steady level)
Maximum number of currency issued:	Not adopted (remained only proposals and not issued; stopped at the suggestion and none were issued)	Not adopted (stopped at the suggestion and none were issued)	Closed (development terminated)	21 million	21 million

Many coins have been generated from bitcoin. Some examples are Bitcoin XT, Bitcoin Unlimited, Bitcoin Classic, Bitcoin Cash and Bitcoin Gold.

Here, an introduction is given to Bitcoin Cash, which may replace bitcoin due to its high level of convenience, such as the speed for transferring money and its handling charges.

Bitcoin Cash (BCH) is a cryptocurrency that was developed when a hard fork was prepared on bitcoin in August 2017. A hard fork is when the old rules for generating new blocks are not applied and, from a certain point, a split occurs in the chronological blockchain. This splits the cryptocurrency completely. It becomes a different blockchain from the previous blockchain, and they will not be linked thereafter. The two blockchains have no compatibility, either. The same volume of bitcoins is issued as at the time of the split, and the maximum number of issues is 21 million, the same as for bitcoin.

The problem of bitcoin splitting was whether to increase the block size (data allowable upper limit) per block. Remuneration obtained by mining is reduced by half once every four years in order to maintain the balance between demand and supply and increase the value of bitcoins. On the other hand, enlarging the block size implies that the amount of data stored in it also increases, which means that the amount of data to be approved increases and the commission increases accordingly. Due to these circumstances, conflicts have arisen over the block size.

A group based in China, where many miners are concentrated, broke away from bitcoin and developed Bitcoin Cash. The block size for Bitcoin Cash became bigger than that for bitcoin. Whereas the block size for bitcoin is 1 MB, the block size for Bitcoin Cash is 8 MB. If the amount of Bitcoin Cash in circulation increases, it will prove the merits of making the block size 8 MB.

Bitcoins became slow and expensive because of the increased time required for their approval along with the rapid increase in transaction volume. That had been because of an increase in the number of blocks that had to be created, since there is a limit to the volume of records that may be stored in a single block. Therefore, when a single block become bigger, the transaction records stored would also increase in quantity, meaning that the speed of processing would become faster. Thus, it was believed that the speed of transfers could be maintained, even if the amount of Bitcoin Cash in circulation and its transaction volumes increased.

Bitcoin Cash came into existence with high expectations; however, it failed at the first hurdle due to the too-high level of difficulty for mining; transaction approvals were not made in ten minutes and inhibited the transactions. The difficulty level of mining was adjusted after that.

The smooth transactions that were conducted after the mining was made less difficult led to a soaring in price. While the price had been around 720 USD to 1 BCH when Bitcoin Cash was first issued with a hard fork in August 2017, it immediately fell to around 180 USD, and then increased to around 450 USD. Once the difficulty of mining had been adjusted, the price soared as high as around 1,350 USD in November 2017, then almost reached 4,500 USD in mid-December 2017. The price of Bitcoin Cash has since been transitioning at around 720 USD, but it has a high rate of volatility.

There has been a lot of positive information on Bitcoin Cash since it appeared on the scene. For example, Britain's CoinEX exchange, which adopted Bitcoin Cash as its key currency, was set up in December 2017, and SBI Virtual Currencies, under the SBI Group, a major financial group in Japan, began handling Bitcoin Cash a week before it introduced bitcoins in June 2018.

An increasing number of companies and stores are starting to accept Bitcoin Cash payments. Because of advantages like its quick speed for transfers, it is possible that demands for Bitcoin Cash may increase in future.

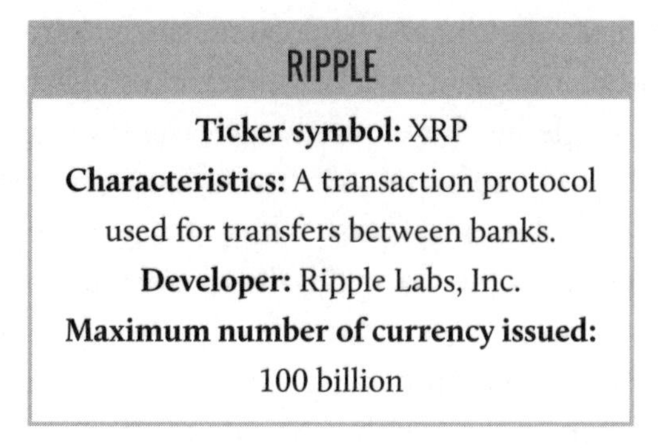

RIPPLE

Ticker symbol: XRP
Characteristics: A transaction protocol used for transfers between banks.
Developer: Ripple Labs, Inc.
Maximum number of currency issued: 100 billion

Ripple has the potential to become another bitcoin – and not in a negative sense. In other words, the price of Ripple could potentially soar.

Ripple is based on a paper that was released by programmer Ryan Fugger in 2004.[2] Unlike bitcoin, which came into being shortly after the release of Satoshi Nakamoto's paper, Ripple did not take shape immediately after the release of the paper.

In August 2012, Ryan Fugger entrusted the Ripple project to a team led by businessman Chris Larsen. Chris Larsen joined the team of Jed McCaleb, who conceived consensus algorithms (a method for approving transactions) and applied them to bitcoin technology in 2011.

Chris Larsen, who took over the Ripple project from Ryan Fugger, founded OpenCoin together with Jed McCaleb (the founder of Mt. Gox) in September 2012.

The ideas that Ryan Fugger and Jed McCaleb conceived merged together, and development began for a protocol called RTXP (Ripple Transaction Protocol). Banks, financial institutions, companies and other organizations throughout the world are considering introducing this system to send and receive currency.

Since then, OpenCoin has changed its name twice – to Ripple Labs in September 2013, then to Ripple in 2015 and RTXP became known throughout the world under the name Ripple network. In addition, Ripple was selected the same year for the Technology Pioneer award, a prize that Google and Twitter have won in the past.

In 2017, an announcement by a special committee (the Faster Payments Task Force) set up by the US Federal Reserve announced RTXP as a faster international payment system for the next generation.

As of April 2018, more than a hundred financial institutions throughout the globe have decided to introduce RTXP.[3] Many companies and organizations, including technology companies, security firms and universities, besides 41 banks, such as the Bank of America, the biggest bank in the USA, and 61 banks in Japan, have announced verification tests and introductions using RTXP.

Ripple's mission is to be an Internet of Value (IoV). The concept of an IoV is to try to make fundamental changes in society by making it possible to conduct exchanges of an array of values (not limited to money) throughout the world in a fast and simple way. There are email protocols for text information such as letters, and it is possible to send email to the entire world in a fast and easy manner. However, no protocol has been invented for sending value (money).

In 2013, Ripple (Ripple Labs at the time) had already guessed the problems that bitcoin would later face, including delays in sending money and expensive handling charges. With these issues in mind, Ripple was developed as a faster, lower-cost system (cryptocurrency). With Ripple's centralized structure, it is possible to make improvements quickly should an issue arise with the system.

Transfers of money using the Ripple system are completed in three to four seconds and may be used 24/7. Ripple is said to be capable of reducing remittance costs for banks and financial institutions by 60%, and an announcement was made in May 2018 that it had succeeded in a 40–70% cost reduction with a pilot version for Ripple's international money transfer system called xRapid (a protocol for businesses that send money).

The distributed ledger used at Ripple is called XRP Ledger. In blockchain, which is a distributed ledger used by bitcoin and Ethereum, transactions are approved by participants in networks of large, unspecified numbers. But with Ripple's XRP Ledger, approval work for transactions is done not by unspecified numbers of participants but by a small number of participants, who are called validators. This is the reason why Ripple said to be centralized.

It is not possible for anyone to become a validator. Only validators who are selected from a Unique Node List (UNL) administered by Ripple are given authority to verify the ledger (blocks within the blockchain).

As mentioned earlier, although Ripple is spreading as a remittance system between banks, there are a few stores at the moment that use it as a payment system. However, in May 2018, Integrated Device Technology, Inc., a US company that supplies communication and payment services, and Mercury FX, an international payment services group, announced an alliance with Ripple. They asserted that they would introduce xRapid to speed up payments for individual remittances and for transactions between companies.

In these ways, it is possible that the number of countries, regions, companies and stores that can use Ripple for payments may further increase, as in the case of bitcoin, in the future, in which case Ripple's value will further increase.

Ripple's value had been hovering between 0.2 and 0.3 USD to 1 XPR around May 2017, and it rose to around 2.7 USD to 1 XRP in January 2018. As of mid-August 2018, its value has fallen to around 0.26 USD.

COMPANIES THAT USE RIPPLE'S REMITTANCE SYSTEM*

Visa	MUFG Bank	Argentaria
American Express	New York Stock Exchange	Nasdaq
Fiserv	United States Ski and Snowboard Association	Goldman Sachs
New York Life	Canadian Imperial Bank of Commerce	Citibank, N.A.
Mastercard	Wedbush Securities	Capital One Financial
Mitsui Sumitomo Insurance Group Holdings	Banco Bilbao Vizcaya	Santander InnoVentures
Transamerica Corporation		and others

COMPANIES THAT INVEST IN RIPPLE*

Google Ventures	Andreessen Horowitz	InnoVentures
Accenture Technology Ventures (Accenture)	CME Group (CME Ventures)	Standard Chartered Bank
SBI Holdings (SBI Group)	Core Innovation Capital	Seagate Technology (Seagate)
	Santander	and others

*As of August 2018
Source: https://ripple.com/company/

ETHEREUM

Ticker symbol: ETH

Characteristics: Smart contracts that enable decentralized administration of transaction contract details and transaction conditions, etc., in addition to transactions.

Number issued: No maximum limit

Among other cryptocurrencies that may be described as representative of the field is Ethereum. It is known as Ethereum but was formally called Ether. As of May 2018, the market capitalization of Ethereum was second to that of bitcoin.

Vitalik Buterin is a Russian-Canadian who conceived Ethereum (ETH) in 2013 when he was only 19. Development began in 2014, and presale (ICO) was initiated in July the same year.

As of August 2018, 110 million ETH have been issued, and currently there is no maximum limit on issues, although Buterin himself suggested in April that a maximum limit be established.

It was at the time of a hacking incident and an uproar over division that Ethereum captured the most attention. An incident occurred in June 2016 where Ethereum was hacked via the cryptocurrency DAO (Decentralized Autonomous Organization), which was generated from Ethereum. DAOs are tokens that were issued for a project that itself used an Ethereum smart contract and was called DAO/The DAO. The amount in losses was 3.6 million ETH, worth approximately 4,695 USD at the time.

This incident ended with the hacked system being rolled back (going back to the state prior to an incident when an incident such as a malfunction occurs to a system, also called a reverse return) and hard forked. Ethereum Classic was developed as a split during that hard fork.

A characteristic of Ethereum is the smart contracts that are linked to the blockchain. With conventional systems, procedures at a public notary's office are necessary to make documents such as a contract official. But by using a smart contract, it is impossible to alter the details in a document that has been uploaded onto the internet. As all histories will be retained if the details are changed, the fairness of a contract is guaranteed without the need to use a public notary's office.

In years to come, smart contracts will not only be used for cryptocurrency but also for various other activities in business, such as in the registration of real estate and the management of resident cards, medical records, supply chains, sharing services and so on.

As Ethereum is a cryptocurrency ranked second after bitcoin in market capitalization, more companies and stores are expected to introduce it as payment. Ethereum is a cryptocurrency that will see more and more improvements in infrastructure, etc. Once it starts to spread, chances are that its value will also increase.

The value of Ethereum transitioned at around 1 USD to 1 ETH since its release in 2014 and gradually rose around January 2016. It came close to 20 USD to 1 ETH in June 2016 at the time of the hacking incident. No notable price declines have occurred since the hacking incident, and the value has been hovering between 12 USD and 15 USD. Ethereum's value began to increase in March 2017 and rose to 391 USD in June 2017. Ethereum is possibly one of the few examples of success after an ICO.

WHAT ARE THE DIFFERENCES BETWEEN THE THREE CRYPTOCURRENCIES?

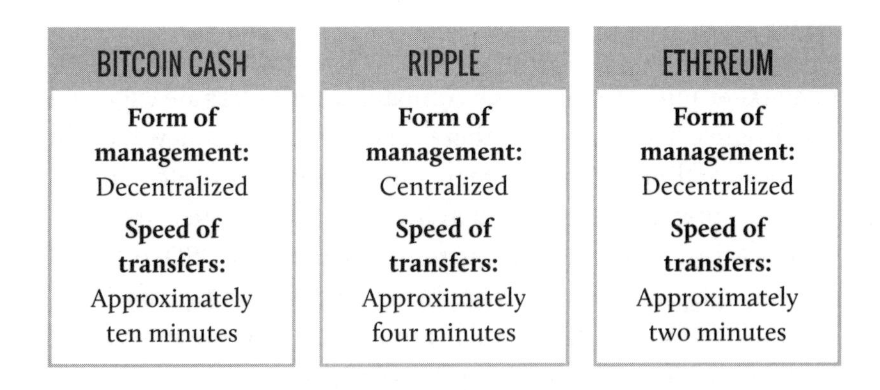

BITCOIN CASH	RIPPLE	ETHEREUM
Form of management: Decentralized	**Form of management:** Centralized	**Form of management:** Decentralized
Speed of transfers: Approximately ten minutes	**Speed of transfers:** Approximately four minutes	**Speed of transfers:** Approximately two minutes

All of the cryptocurrencies introduced – Bitcoin Cash, Ripple and Ethereum – are different. The differences are chiefly between the:

- Form of management
- Speed of transfers
- Basis for reliability

Forms of management for cryptocurrencies can be broken down into two types: decentralized and centralized. Bitcoin Cash and Ethereum are decentralized, and Ripple is centralized.

FORM OF MANAGEMENT

A decentralized form of management means an absence of a representative individual who has the right to control a cryptocurrency, and is used as having the opposite meaning to a centralized form of management.

A P2P system is used, where functions are distributed between multiple computers or a function is made to work through a distribution. Bitcoin uses this decentralized architecture. The advantage of a decentralized system is that participants in the network are free to present ideas and improve themselves. The disadvantage is that responses are delayed when issues arise and there is no one to sort through the different opinions and ideas.

On the other hand, a centralized system means there is a representative who has the right to control things, although control in the world of cryptocurrency is not like intervention that there is in FX. A structure is in place in which improvements may be made by the issuing party when a problem arises with the system, such as a delay in the transfer of funds.

The advantage of a centralized cryptocurrency is that the representative can immediately take steps when a problem arises. That person can take actions in the event of malicious intent that will result in a significant loss for the user. This can be seen, however, to be a disadvantage in that it has the potential to lead to a 'dictatorship'.

However, because cryptocurrency began in a decentralized form, like bitcoin, it is also sometimes said that centralized cryptocurrencies are not cryptocurrencies.

THE SPEED OF SENDING MONEY

The speed of sending money varies depending on the cryptocurrency. Bitcoin is said to take around ten minutes because of the authentication time required for the transaction. Next, it takes four seconds to send Ripple, and it takes about two minutes to send Ethereum.

THE FOUNDATION OF TRUST

Trust secures the safety of a cryptocurrency. With decentralized cryptocurrencies like Bitcoin Cash and Ethereum, the people who participate in the cryptocurrency networks secure safety for each other. The network exists in the foundation of reliability.

Still, for centralized cryptocurrencies as well, whether reliability exists amid many users may become an indicator to measure the reliability of the cryptocurrency in itself. However, for a case like that, there is first a need to learn about the issuing party.

For example, Ripple is the party that issues Ripple cryptocurrency. For that reason, it is possible to check information such as the company's performance, its financial status, business plans, biographies of managers and management, the companies that it invests in, and the companies that it deals with from the information it discloses.

If you are considering a cryptocurrency as something to invest in, it is therefore desirable to thoroughly study how that currency can be categorized and to understand its characteristics before selecting it for investment.

ARE THERE DIFFERENCES IN THE REGULATIONS FOR CRYPTOCURRENCY TRANSACTIONS?

USA (STATE OF NEW YORK)	GREAT BRITAIN	FRANCE
BitLicense (approval) required for cryptocurrency-related businesses.	Licence required for businesses that conduct futures trading, contracts for difference (CFDs) or options trading.	Policy to introduce a licensing system for exchanges in accordance with EU regulations.

RUSSIA	JAPAN
Legislative system being prepared to restrict transactions.	Licence from Financial Services Agency required for exchanges.

SOUTH KOREA / ICOS	BRAZIL
Are prohibited.	Domestic investment funds are prohibited from buying cryptocurrency.

Regulations concerning cryptocurrency vary greatly from country to country. Some countries are enthusiastic about introducing cryptocurrency, while others are moving to eliminate it. In either case, the increasing recognition of cryptocurrency has prompted countries to take steps towards regulation.

In the USA, the compilation of rules and regulations is underway in each state. For example, in the state of Washington, businesses associated with cryptocurrency trading are required to obtain a licence from the state's department of financial institutions.[4] In addition to being required to submit the personal information of users as needed, it is mandatory for a cryptocurrency exchange to compensate for damage in the event that trouble occurs in the transmission of money and to secure a reserve fund for protecting users in accordance with the volume of transactions. On the other hand, in the state of New York, it has now become mandatory to obtain a BitLicense issued by the New York State Department of Financial Services in order to manage or issue cryptocurrency or to offer transmission and management services. As for New Hampshire, the state has announced that it will not tax cryptocurrency transactions that use blockchain, showing that some states support the spread of cryptocurrency.

Great Britain has taken an open-minded position to date with regard to cryptocurrency. However, Prime Minister Theresa May expressed concern at the World Economic Forum held in January 2018 that bitcoin and other cryptocurrencies were being used for criminal activities and that the government had to look very seriously at monitoring such moves.[5] In response, Philip Hammond, the Chancellor of the Exchequer, launched a select committee on cryptocurrency and began to introduce regulations.

The Financial Conduct Authority (FCA) of Britain announced a statement with the following information on its website:

- Cryptocurrencies are not currently regulated by the FCA.
- However, 'encryption currency derivatives' can be regarded as financial instruments. Therefore, it can be subject to EU second financial instruments market directive (MiFID 2).
- Firms conducting regulated activities in cryptocurrency derivatives must comply with applicable rules in the FCA guidelines in addition to any relevant provisions in applicable EU regulations.
- Any services such as those mentioned provided by cryptocurrency service providers who have not received authorization by the FCA will be considered criminal acts.
- The provision of similar services without appropriate authorization may be applicable for compulsory enforcement (by the FCA) regardless of whether the pertinent party is an authorized service provider.

Furthermore, Britain takes the position that regulations are necessary, not only in its own country but on a global scale, and is calling for France and Germany to also impose regulations.

In France, Minister of the Economy Bruno Le Maire announced in mid-January 2018 the establishment of a cryptocurrency research team. And in February 2018, France's Financial Markets Authority (AMF) announced a policy that cryptocurrency exchanges were to operate under a licensing system.[6]

Le Mail contributed to Webmedia's Nemermama (Numerama.com) specialization in French digital and high-tech industry. "No consumer, bank depositor or entrepreneur can carry out a transaction, can invest or can develop a business in a regulatory vacuum," and offered the assessment that "A revolution is underway, of which Bitcoin was only the precursor. The blockchain will offer new opportunities to our start-ups, for example with the initial coin offerings for procuring funds using 'tokens'".[7]

While the purpose of the creation of the research team is said to be to control tax evasion, money laundering and other illegal uses, it has shown a basic stance of recognizing the future potential of cryptocurrency while incorporating regulations for maintaining order.

In Russia, federal legislation was submitted in March 2018 to establish regulations on cryptocurrency trading. Rather than introducing general regulations for cryptocurrency, it authorizes transactions and ICOs under certain criteria. The Russian finance ministry is of the position that a general prohibition of cryptocurrency would create a hotbed of crime, such as illegal businesses, money laundering and funding for terrorist activities. The finance ministry expects a reduction in the risk of fraud and other crimes and tax revenue from cryptocurrency transactions.

In Switzerland, major financial institutions are starting to deal with bitcoin investments. Specifically, Falcon Private Bank and Swissquote, which offers online banking services, announced in July 2017 that they would become the first financial institutions in Switzerland to advance into the cryptocurrency business.

"While many investors are interested in cryptocurrency, they have concerns when it comes to transactions. It's because they don't know much about market participants, and they are often sought to transfer funds to foreign accounts. As a Swiss bank, we will offer services with a high level of transparency that anyone can use through simple procedures without the need to send money abroad," said Swissquote CEO Marc Burki.[8]

Furthermore, the opening of an account for a cryptocurrency/blockchain-related company by Hypothekarbank Lenzburg in June 2018 also gained the spotlight.

In Estonia, in August 2017 it was announced that a cryptocurrency called estcoin would be issued by the government. Estonia is known as the birthplace of the free telecommunications application Skype, and with the development of IT identified as a national policy, it is also aggressive with regard to cryptocurrency.

As mentioned earlier, an amended Payment Services Act took effect in Japan on 1 April 2017, and the definition of what is called virtual currency and what is referred to as a virtual currency exchange service was established by law. Authorization by and registration with the Financial Services Agency became necessary to operate an exchange.

In Hong Kong, the Securities and Futures Commission (SFC) announced in September 2017 that cryptocurrency exchanges and ICOs would require closer monitoring.[9] Thus, several ICOs in Hong Kong were regarded by the SFC as being collective investment schemes[10] and became required to meet pertinent standards. It is necessary for ICOs to receive advance inspection and to register in order to accept investors. ICOs that had not been taking these steps were ordered to suspend business in March of the same year.[11]

In South Korea, the Financial Services Commission (FSC) announced a ban on all ICOs as "risk of fraud" in August 2017.[12] It also said it would forbid credit transactions of cryptocurrencies. The FSC stressed that the South Korean government intended to monitor the situation and improve future regulatory control because a bill to legalize domestic ICO was submitted to the Diet at the end of May 2017.

In January 2018, the Brazilian government announced that it would ban domestic investment funds from investing directly in cryptocurrencies.[13] The Securities and Exchange Commission of Brazil (CVM), which regulates cryptocurrency-related businesses such as exchanges, banned domestic investment funds from buying cryptocurrency and made it mandatory for exchanges to adhere to its anti-money-laundering law.

ARE THERE COUNTRIES THAT HAVE BANNED CRYPTOCURRENCIES?

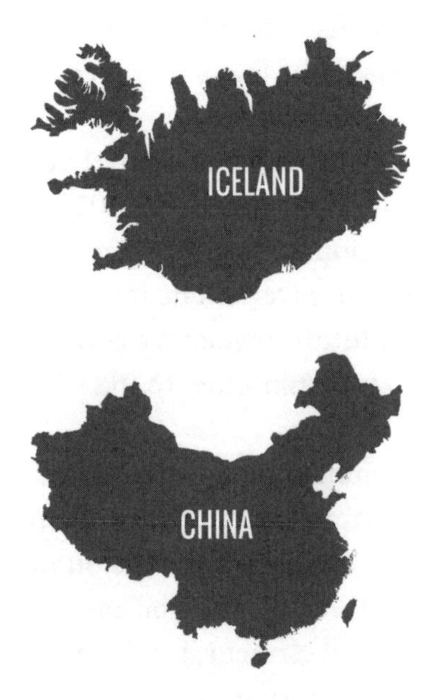

There is a total ban on the buying and selling of cryptocurrency. Circulation is only allowed for (cryptocurrency) mined in the country.

Cryptocurrency trading and the issuing of tokens (ICOs) is prohibited, both within and outside the country.

There are countries where cryptocurrency trading is prohibited. They include Iceland and China.

After being severely impacted by the financial crisis of 2008, Iceland experienced a rapid comeback through the government's tough austerity measures. From the standpoint of preventing capital outflow, the Central Bank of Iceland in 2014 announced that it would not allow foreign currency to be taken out of the country through the use of bitcoins.[14] However, the ownership of bitcoins and the mining of bitcoins are, in fact, accepted.[15] The release of Auroracoin – a peer-to-peer cryptocurrency launched in February 2014 as an Icelandic alternative to bitcoin – became a topic of discussion among citizens. Furthermore, there were also reports that many mining companies were attracted to the cold weather and the wealth of electricity from geothermal power generation, and that in February 2018, the consumption of electric power from mining exceeded consumption in homes. These things are seen as impacting the taxation system on profits obtained from mining in the future.[16]

In China, the ban on cryptocurrency trading and the issuing of tokens (ICOs) by Chinese users was announced in September 2017.[17] The regulatory authorities in China said they would implement a series of regulatory steps for cryptocurrency transactions and ICOs in China and abroad. Steps include a crackdown on commercial bases and a crackdown on any dealing with cryptocurrency exchanges in and outside China, with the regulatory authorities adding that they would make companies and organizations that were in violation close down as soon as they were found.

Around the same time as these reports came out in China, advertisements related to cryptocurrency and ICOs disappeared from Baidu, a major player in China for online searches, and Weibo, the Chinese version of Twitter. It is said that articles stopped being found when conducting key-word searches such as for 'bitcoin', 'cryptocurrency' ('virtual currency') and 'ICO'.

Chinese users may, however, be conducting transactions in Hong Kong, where cryptocurrency trading is not prohibited.

ARE THERE DIFFERENCES IN THE TAX SYSTEMS FOR CRYPTOCURRENCY?

USA

Capital gains taxes are applied.

GREAT BRITAIN

There are no taxes when cryptocurrencies and pounds are exchanged.

A 20% value-added tax is applied when goods or services are purchased with cryptocurrency.

Income tax, corporate tax and capital gains tax are applied to profits obtained through cryptocurrency transactions.

FRANCE

A 19% tax is applicable to all cryptocurrency sales.

RUSSIA

A 13% tax is applicable to cryptocurrency sales.

HONG KONG

None.

JAPAN

Taxes applicable as miscellaneous income (5–45%)

BRAZIL

A 15% tax is applicable when sales revenue exceeds 35,000 real per month.

The treatment of cryptocurrency with regard to tax systems varies from country to country. While the rules for cryptocurrency trading are gradually being developed in different countries, there are a surprisingly small number of countries where tax systems have been established. It may be said that tax systems are still in the early stages of consideration.

In 2014, the Internal Revenue Service (IRS), the revenue service of the US federal government which enforces and collects federal taxes, announced how cryptocurrency would be handled in terms of income tax:[18]

- The buying, selling, trading or exchanging of cryptocurrencies for goods or services, will be subject to tax.
- Cryptocurrency will be treated as an asset in the same way as securities.
- Market value at the time that a cryptocurrency is obtained will be used for calculating taxes (also applicable for cryptocurrency obtained from mining).

In the USA, capital gains tax is applicable to revenue earned from cryptocurrency. Capital gains tax refers to a tax on profit obtained through a change in the price of a capital asset such as a stock. A preferential treatment system exists in the USA whereby the tax rate reduces when an asset is owned for a period that exceeds a year. When an asset is owned for less than one year, a 10–39.8% tax rate is applicable. When an asset is owned for a period exceeding one year, a tax rate of 0, 15 or 20% is applicable.

In Britain, while an exchange between cryptocurrency and the pound will not be subject to tax, the sale of goods or services using cryptocurrency will be subject to a 20% value-added tax. Profit obtained through cryptocurrency transactions will be subject to income tax, corporate tax or capital gains tax,[19] depending on the situation.

In France, the Council of State (a government advisory body) has changed the tax rate on the sale of cryptocurrency from more than 45% to date to 19% across the board.[20] This is a result of a new tax category for differentiating between commercial and non-commercial activities. There is an awareness that in principle the sale of cryptocurrencies constitutes capital gains on moving property. Revenue from mining is taxed as non-commercial profit. As for profits from specialized activities, these are taxed as industrial or commercial profits.

In Russia, a proposal for a new law on digital financial assets is being discussed, and the tax system will be revised accordingly. As for the tax system concerning cryptocurrency until then, the finance ministry has issued a statement to the effect that the tax rate for gains from trading cryptocurrencies like bitcoin is 13%.[21]

In Japan, an amended Payment Services Act came into force in July 2017. Cryptocurrencies became exempt from consumption tax, as they were not recognized as objects but in practice as currencies that have the same type of financial value as standard currencies. The profits gained from the sale of cryptocurrencies are categorized as miscellaneous income in principle and subject to comprehensive taxation .[22]

The tax rate is a progressive tax in combination with a standard 10% residents' tax, and a total tax rate of 15–55% (maximum tax rate) is applicable in accordance with the amount of income. The tax rates for different income levels are as follows:

- Less than 1.95 million yen – 5%
- 1.95 to 3.3 million yen – 10%
- 3.3 to 6.95 million yen – 20%
- 6.95–9 million yen – 23%
- 9–18 million yen – 33%
- 18–40 million yen – 40%
- More than 40 million yen – 45%

In Hong Kong, no special examples of the tax system are currently established concerning cryptocurrency. Interest tax, dividend tax and capital gains tax were abolished in 1989, and taxes currently exist for general corporate tax (about 16.5%) and income tax (standard rate 15%; maximum rate 17%).

There is an obligation to report the ownership of cryptocurrency in Brazil, and a tax system like the following is in place for capital gains from cryptocurrency:[23]

- Cryptocurrency exceeding 5,000 real must be reported as an asset each year when tax returns are filed.
- A 15% tax (the same rate as capital gains) must be paid when monthly profit on sales exceeds 35,000 real.

Tax structures will certainly be established in other countries as well in the future. Various rules on buying and selling cryptocurrency and businesses associated with cryptocurrency are certain to be moved forward as well.

ARE THERE WITHDRAWAL LIMITS IN SOME COUNTRIES?

Depending on the country, there are times when restrictions are imposed when you withdraw profits obtained from cryptocurrency investments. Such restrictions are probably a measure for preventing money laundering and other such acts.

Other than having rules pertaining to cryptocurrency, there are also countries that impose special restrictions with regard to international money transfers, and unique rules are in place at individual banks or financial institutions concerning international transfers. Thus, you may experience some inconvenience when withdrawing a certain amount of cash or when sending money overseas, even when the country imposes no regulations or restrictions on withdrawals.

For example, let's say that you are going to stay overseas for several months. You're going to rent a house, and you have to send four months' rent at the outset. The rent is around 10,000 USD. You go to a nearby commercial bank to make an international transfer. The procedures for sending money are completed that day, and you believe that the money will be received by the other party in a few days. But you are asked to present documents such as the following and to contact (the bank) a week before your remittance:

- Identification
- Documents to prove your association with the recipient
- Identification for the recipient
- Documents to prove where the money you're sending came from (a copy of your bank passbook for the last six months as well as the original)

You have no choice but to go home, prepare the necessary documents and go back to the bank the following week. Five days after you began the procedures, the money transfer arrived at its destination.

This is something that actually happened to me.

Furthermore, when sending money not as an individual but as a company, you may be required to present things like your articles of incorporation and company registration. In addition, if the recipient is a company, there is no doubt that documents like invoices will be necessary.

While this is an example of a bank with particularly tough rules, I do have a sense that procedures, particularly for international money transfers, are becoming more complicated. There are also banks that have a limit on the amount of individual or annual remittances.

In addition, the exchange contacted me and asked that I prepare the necessary documents and personal identification required for making the withdrawal. The withdrawal was not easy, and there was a lot of waiting, so I asked what limitation was being incurred on the withdrawal of profit obtained from investing in cryptocurrency. With no other choice, I sent the cryptocurrency to a Swiss exchange and withdrew from there to a designated bank account. Limitations on withdrawals and transfers are very inconvenient when the assets are supposed to be yours. I think is necessary to do whatever it takes to eliminate such inconveniences.

DO OTHER PROMISING CRYPTOCURRENCIES EXIST?

There are promising cryptocurrencies besides Bitcoin Cash, Ripple and Ethereum. They include Fusion Coin, Litecoin, New Economic Movement (NEM) and Dash.

FUSION COIN
Form of management: Centralized
Ticker symbol: XFC
Number issued: 30 million

Fusion Coin was created in 2015 by a team comprising various nationalities, including French and Japanese. This cryptocurrency is issued by a company called Fusion Partners, and Roger Ver is a key advisor.

Fusion Coin is made using Ripple's IOUs (electronic bonds that can be exchanged for cryptocurrency). By using Ripple's highly reliable transfer system, exchanges to currencies throughout the world are possible quickly.

Sales of Fusion Coin began in January 2016. Negotiated transactions began in early 2017, and trading has become such that people are now free to conduct buying and selling as they wish. While the rate had been 1.9 USD to 1 XFC at the time of initial sales, it came close to 20 USD in February 2018. All price fluctuations in the past may be seen on an exchange site that is directly operated by Fusion Partners.

Litecoin was issued in 2011 as a cryptocurrency specifically for settlements and fund transfers. Charlie Lee, a former Google engineer, developed it as an improvement of bitcoin.

LITECOIN
Form of management: Decentralized
Ticker symbol: LTC
Number issued: 84 million

As mentioned, up to this point there had been issues with bitcoin: chiefly, a slow speed of transfer and high service charges. The Litecoin cryptocurrency was developed to resolve these issues and is said to be more practical compared with bitcoin. While transfers of bitcoins take an average of ten minutes and at times several hours, it takes only two or three minutes to transfer Litecoins. In addition, while it depends on conditions, the handling fee for sending money is around 0.3 USD for Litecoin compared with about 20 USD for bitcoins.

The practicality that Litecoin offers means that it was anticipated to be used for making payments. As of summer 2018, plans were made for issuing debit cards called LitePay and for developing LitePal, a cryptocurrency version of the PayPal payment system.

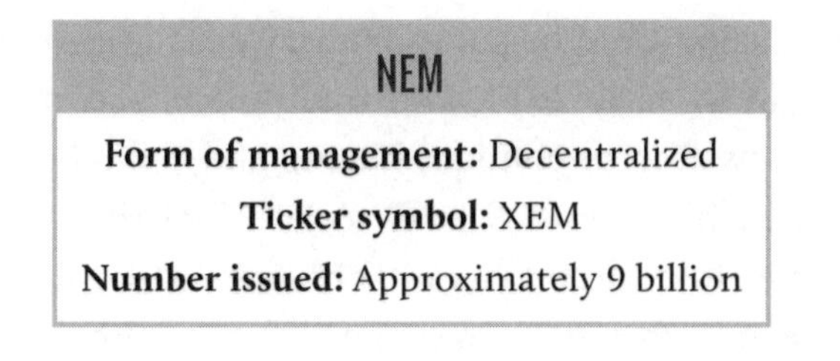

NEM

Form of management: Decentralized

Ticker symbol: XEM

Number issued: Approximately 9 billion

NEM is a cryptocurrency that was developed in a project aimed to create an equal, decentralized platform. In aiming to resolve the uneven distribution of wealth, Proof of Importance (POI) is used as an algorithm. POI aims to become a new economic framework that isn't inhibited by conventional economic frameworks. POI is a framework that considers the level of importance with things like the volume of coins possessed by participants and the frequency of their transactions that provide remuneration from mining. However, as the maximum number of NEM have already been issued by NEM, remuneration is paid not with newly issued coins but as handling fees.

There is a strong community of die-hard fans of NEM, called NEMbers, who conduct various activities to try to spread NEM. There are nemket markets where NEM may be used to make payments, the market site nemche has been established, and also NEM bars where alcoholic drinks may be enjoyed and paid for using NEM.

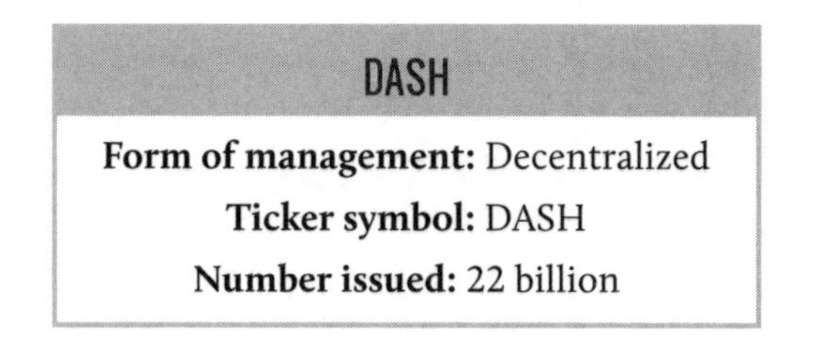
DASH

Form of management: Decentralized
Ticker symbol: DASH
Number issued: 22 billion

Dash was developed with the objective of promoting its use for payments in virtual space in the same way that cash is used. The total number of issues is 22 billion, and Dash has been set up so that 7.1% will be newly issued on an annual basis. Dash was disclosed in January 2014, and although it was called X Coin at the outset, it passed through the name of dark coin and became a dash in 2015.

The beneficial characteristics of Dash are its speed of transfers and the anonymity at the time that a transfer is made. Dash may be sent in approximately 1.3 seconds, and is said to be suitable for making payments. As to anonymity, third parties are able to see transaction histories for bitcoins due to the nature of the blockchain that supports it, but with Dash, a black box called a pool is set up between the sender and the recipient to secure anonymity. No records remain of the transfer from party A to party B, and the framework is such that only the information that money had been sent to the pool and received from the pool is left as transaction history.

In 2017 the value of Dash increased significantly. While 1 DASH had been around 10 USD in January 2017, it increased to 540 USD in November and 1,500 USD in December 2017.

The value of cryptocurrencies changes in real time. Prices and aggregate market prices may be checked on CoinMarketCap and CoinCap. Although these are only information sites, cryptocurrencies that are not listed on the sites are sometimes called scam coins. However, a cryptocurrency that is listed on an information site like CoinMarketCap is not necessarily a cryptocurrency that you can safely invest in.

WHICH ARE THE MOST PROMISING CRYPTOCURRENCIES?

Among the many new cryptocurrencies, Fusion Coin is the cryptocurrency that has the best potential for an increase in value. The five main bases for that are as follows:

- The total number of issues is small
- It offers fast speeds of transfers
- Service charges are low
- It's easy to make withdrawals
- It has a high degree of security

The small number of issues affects volatility. The reason the value of bitcoins rose from 8 cents to 18,000 USD was because the total number of issues had been set. The total number of Fusion Coins issued is 30 million, which is small in comparison to the volume of many other cryptocurrencies that exist.

As an example to explain the pricing of cryptocurrencies, consider the sale of motor vehicles. Imagine that a car manufacturer has produced a car in limited numbers with good features and a good overall design. Only 100 of these cars are produced. The price is set at 100,000 USD, but 1,000 people want to buy the car, including some who say they will pay 1 million USD. As the popularity of the car increases, the initial price of 100,000 USD rises to 1 million USD and potentially even more, maybe to 10 million USD. And in the end, the cars may to be sold for around 12 million USD.

The reason for the increased value of bitcoins is similar to this example. If the total number of issues is predetermined, the price will rise as cryptocurrency's popularity increases. Conversely, a large number of issues will lower this kind of price volatility.

Fast speeds of transfer significantly affect the degree of convenience. On average, the transfer of bitcoins takes ten minutes, Ethereum takes two minutes and Fusion Coin takes only a few seconds.

Is it possible to use a cryptocurrency that has slow transfer speeds for payments? Imagine a scenario where you're using cryptocurrency to make a payment. You're at the till and you're about to pay. You transfer bitcoins from your wallet, but the transfer isn't completed even after ten minutes. It would take at least two minutes with Ethereum. You have to stand at the till and wait until the transfer process is complete. A fast transfer is therefore extremely important in order to boost the level of convenience.

Low rates of service charges affect the spread of a cryptocurrency. Whether the fee is for a transfer or for buying or selling, people will not want to use the cryptocurrency frequently if the pricing is high. The service charge for a bitcoin transfer is around 0.0001–0.001 BTC, depending on how the prices are set up, but it will vary by a few dollars depending on the bitcoin rate. While the handling charge for buying and selling will vary from one exchange to another, it's around 0.01– 0.15%. Some exchanges offer free handling (i.e. no fees) during a special campaign.

The handling fee in the case of Fusion Coin is 0.001% for transfers and 0.0005% for buying and selling. This means the sending fee for 10,000 USD is only 0.1 USD and around 0.05 USD for trading.

Furthermore, the ease in making withdrawals affects the degree of convenience. A surprisingly small number of cryptocurrencies can be cashed directly. Many cryptocurrencies may only be traded (matched) with bitcoins, which can be referred to as a key cryptocurrency, and only withdrawn using bitcoins. To convert such a cryptocurrency to cash, it is necessary to take the following steps:

1. The cryptocurrency must be converted to bitcoins.
2. Bitcoins are matched with and converted to US dollars.
3. The US dollars are transferred to a designated account.

In other words, you first need to get your cryptocurrency exchanged to bitcoins and then exchange that to cash, and handling fees must be paid each time.

On the other hand, in the case of Fusion Coin, funds may be withdrawn in cash (US dollars), bitcoin, Bitcoin Cash or Ripple. It's also possible to make deposits in cash (US dollars), bitcoin, Bitcoin Cash or Ripple. Fusion Coin should become even more convenient in the future, as there are plans to include more cryptocurrencies in this list.

Lastly, the high degree of security is extremely important. There are two key points with regard to security: first, that individual wallets are managed for each user, and second, that servers are spread out in multiple locations.

Online wallets have the potential of being hacked. Particularly when storing cryptocurrency in a wallet at an exchange, the important thing is how that exchange administers the wallet. While it's fine if a wallet is used to manage each user, there are some exchanges that actually manage one cryptocurrency with a single wallet.

For example, in the 2018 NEM leak incident at the Japanese exchange Coincheck, 58 billion yen's worth of NEM were hacked. This occurred because NEM had been managed in a single wallet. Coincheck had not created individual wallets for each user, and it had been managing the currency with a single wallet, so all NEM stored at the exchange was stolen in one hacking attack.

In contrast, Fusion Coin creates individual wallets for each user. Thus, similar incidents do not occur.

Security measures for servers are also extremely important, because the risks of server malfunctions, natural disasters and hacking increase when only one server is used.

Fusion Coin uses multiple servers. It isn't possible to steal Fusion Coins unless all servers are hacked at the same time, which is realistically impossible.

In these ways, Fusion Coin was developed with considerations made for its high rate of volatility, level of convenience and high level of security.

The fact that Fusion Coin has completed development and the current status enables trading as desired should give investors confidence in its security.

CHAPTER 4

EXPLORING THE POTENTIAL OF INVESTING IN AN ICO

WHAT IS AN ICO (INITIAL COIN OFFERING)?

An ICO – an initial coin offering – is a method for procuring funds using cryptocurrency. An ICO is also called a crowdsale, presale or token sale. The term ICO imitates IPO (initial public offering), which means a new stock issued or a newly listed stock. Ripple's Ripple Fund was the pioneer with ICOs, although at the time these were called funds (the term ICO being used later).

Tokens are issued to a person who invests in an ICO. A token may be understood as being something like a promissory note. Tokens are set up so that when the development of a cryptocurrency has ended and it becomes disclosed, the tokens become that cryptocurrency. In other words, they aren't yet cryptocurrency while they're still tokens. People sometimes think they've bought cryptocurrency because they've invested in an ICO, but that is a misunderstanding.

Ethereum, a symbolic example of a successful ICO, conducted presale from 22 July to 2 September 2014. The rate at the time was 2,000 ETH to 1 BTC. The rate rose as high as about 0.09 ETH to 1 BTC by early 2018. What that means is that Ethereum has multiplied by 180 times in BTC denominations. If the growth rate of BTC during the same period was about 60 times, a simple calculation would mean that Ethereum increased by 10,800 times.

Due to the large number of ICOs being conducted now, it's hard to imagine that something similar will happen again.

In an IPO stock investment, the right to buy stocks is purchased by draw before a new listing, and profit is produced by selling at the stock price (opening price) on the first day of its listing. As discussed later, funds are collected in a similar structure for ICOs, but while stock offerings are made based on the performance of a company and its financial status, no information is disclosed in an ICO on performance or financial status. In some ways, therefore, an IPO and an ICO are essentially different. A document that outlines the business plan, called a white paper, is the only thing that is disclosed in an ICO.

It's fair to say that an ICO is a joint liability structure where everyone takes responsibility. While someone usually takes responsibility for any failures that may ensue when starting a new project or business, in the case of an ICO, everyone who invested takes responsibility. And additionally, these investors have no management rights and they are unable to see the status of management (the status of cryptocurrency development).

Compared with investing in an existing cryptocurrency that may immediately be traded, an investment in an ICO is likely to produce massive profit if it is successful. You may be able to aim for increases in value of several hundred or thousand times. But you must not forget that there is also a risk that the money that you invested will become worth zero, or that the cryptocurrency may not even go so far as to be issued. Depending on how you look at it, the procurement of funds through an ICO may be described as being extremely irresponsible.

ICOs are held by companies and organizations (who call for investment) and are basically open for participation (investment) by anyone. Applications may usually be made online. It's fair to say that ICOs are similar to buying products online.

When choosing an ICO to invest in, the character of the party hosting the ICO (the issuing body for the cryptocurrency) is very important. No matter how excellent the vision or white paper may be, there is the risk that the minute the funds have been accumulated, the individuals may suddenly change. In the case of an ICO, large amounts of funds are accumulated. As an example, is there a chance that a person might change if tens of millions of dollars are suddenly accumulated at once? Still, the mechanism of an ICO is that it may only be left to the morals of the host at the end.

So, why then have ICOs spread to such an extent? It's possible to say that they are only riding on the successes of cryptocurrencies to date. These include the successful case of the soaring value of bitcoin and the successful ICO of Ethereum. Based on these examples of success, the situation is such that the terms ICO and cryptocurrency are being used as tools for procuring funds.

When you want to start a new business, the general method is that a business plan is created, an application is put in for a loan at a bank or a financial institution, or funds are collected from investors through privately placed bonds,[1] or you start your business with your own resources. But recently, perhaps because of the knowledge that fund procurement is easy when an ICO is used, they are being used in increasing numbers to collect funds.

Investing in an ICO shouldn't be a problem if you invest an amount that you can afford to lose.

It is possible to achieve huge gains if you go for further investment in another ICO with a cryptocurrency that has produced profits, depending on the ICO. It is difficult to find a cryptocurrency that will multiply by a thousand times, but it certainly isn't impossible to find one that will increase to five or ten times its value. If it is ten times ten, it becomes hundred times the value.

WHAT IS THE STRUCTURE FOR THE PROCUREMENT OF FUNDS IN AN ICO?

In many ICOs, funds are procured through a method of gathering customers called a product launch. A product launch is a marketing method that was created by a marketer called Jeff Walker.[2] The full name is product launch formula, and it is an online marketing method that looks systematically at the procedures required to produce high sales at the time of a product launch.

More than 4,000 people throughout the world practise product launch based on Jeff Walker's lectures. Marketers have used this method and achieved sales exceeding 5 million USD in 24 hours.

A product launch will bring in customers with a landing page, ezines and videos. The information listed on a landing page is only about the introduction of a project. To obtain further details, there is a need to register an email address; an ezine will then be sent on a regular basis with more information.

There are no elements of sales pitches in the ezines. Instead, they print only information that will be useful to readers and information of value that they are likely to be interested in. Ezines also use videos to give recipients a better understanding. Because of that, many people start to trust the organizer little by little as these steps are taken.

The steps for a product launch are as follows:

1. Prepare a landing page for the product. Use tools like SEOs, portal sites, affiliates and personal information (email addresses) obtained from venders to attract potential customers to the landing page.
2. Obtain the email addresses of potential customers on the landing page.
3. Distribute ezines to the email addresses that have been obtained. Place emphasis on the first email and attract interest from potential customers.
4. Eliminate sales promotion elements; supply a small amount of valuable information at a time to educate potential customers.
5. Launch and sell the product after building a trusting relationship with potential customers through the ezine and videos.

HOW DO YOU INVEST IN AN ICO?

The methods for investing in ICOs will vary for each project organizer (issuing party). While there are some ICOs where funding is possible through cash, there are also those that it is only possible to invest in with bitcoins and so forth.

For example, Ethereum is a symbolic cryptocurrency that was developed through an ICO, and it was only possible to invest in it with bitcoins. There may, however, have been occasions where someone mediated for a purchase using cash or another cryptocurrency. There are often cases, like bitcoin, where ICOs have a predetermined number of issues. And in the same way as with investments, there are times when withdrawals may only be made in cryptocurrency, in which case the cryptocurrency obtained through an ICO must be exchanged for something like bitcoins, which are then sold to enable a cash withdrawal or else used as a payment, with a type of buffer in the process.

A friend of mine, who I will refer to as person N, has been investing in ICOs since around 2015. I heard that he injected funds into something that used a product launch and made a call for investors; as a result, he made approximately ten times what he had invested in roughly just one year.

Person N said he saw the landing page, registered his email address, and received an ezine and video in a couple of weeks or so, after which several briefings and study sessions were held. He told me that it was possible to apply for investments at the briefings back then, and it was also possible to register through the online site or by email. The procedures were simple, and he said all he had to do was provide basic contact information like his name and address and indicate how much of a stake he wanted to invest in (10 USD per token). After that, he said the latest rates were published once a week on the member site. The rate rose to 100 USD about a year later.

To sell the tokens, all person N had to do was enter his name and address, the number of tokens, and the recipient to whom he would send cryptocurrency in the designated form. Handling charges were about 20% of the profit, and the amount after subtracting the handling fee was deposited to the designated account.

The procedures were quite simple. But today, because some countries regulate transactions concerning ICOs and cryptocurrencies, as mentioned earlier, limitations exist in some countries and regions for deposits and withdrawals. That's something that requires attention.

ARE THERE SUCCESS STORIES WITH REGARD TO ICOs?

ETHEREUM
Characteristics: Smart contracts enable decentralized administration of data, e.g. details of a transaction agreement or terms of a transaction as well as transactions.
Procured amount: Just short of around 15 million USD
Value: More than approximately 9,000 times the value at the time of presale

There are several successful cases with ICOs. Specifically, Ethereum, EOS and OmiseGO are examples. The most famous case of a successful ICO is Ethereum. Ethereum issued the token Ether and began sales to investors in September 2014. The term ICO didn't exist at the time, and it was called funding.

Funding for Ethereum was only possible in bitcoins, and 31,529 BTC were collected from around the world. Converting the bitcoins with the exchange rate at the time of 480 USD to 1 BTC, this represents almost 15 million USD in procurement funds.

Although the value may be a little difficult to understand because of the matching with bitcoins, presale for Ethereum began by exchanging 2,000 ETH for 1 BTC.

After starting at 0.0005 BTC to 1 ETH, which was about 0.18 USD (September 2014), Ethereum posted 0.008 BTC to 1 ETH (30 July 2015) after it was issued. It was a rise in value of about 16 times in approximately 10 months.

After several ups and downs since, the value of Ethereum can now be matched against the US dollar. The value of Ethereum posted a record 1,656 USD on 10 January 2018, more than 9,000 times its value at presale.

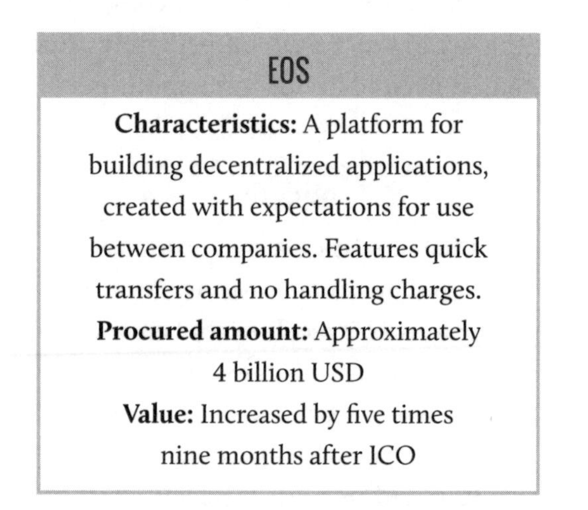

EOS

Characteristics: A platform for building decentralized applications, created with expectations for use between companies. Features quick transfers and no handling charges.

Procured amount: Approximately 4 billion USD

Value: Increased by five times nine months after ICO

EOS is a cryptocurrency where a billion tokens have been issued since its release, with the ticker symbol EOS. An ICO was announced on 26 June 2017, and tokens were issued between 1 July 2017 and 1 June 2018, aiming for the procurement of funds for software development.

EOS was developed by a company called Block.one, based in the Cayman Islands. Block.one has around 200 employees in places like Hong Kong, California and Virginia, and it is a startup company that develops business solutions related to blockchain.

EOS is a platform for building decentralized applications and is planned for broad use between companies. It has two characteristics: the fast speed of transfers and the lack of service charges.

With EOS, the speed of processing information (transactions), starting with transfers of funds, is quite fast. And on top of that, there are no service charges for transactions.

Approximately 4 billion USD was procured for EOS during the year after July 2017. The value of EOS after its issue, which had exceeded approximately 4 USD to 1 EOS immediately after its ICO, plummeted as low as 0.5 USD in October 2017. The value recovered the next month and rose to 10 USD in January 2018, and then to 20 USD in April 2018. When comparing EOS's value in 2018 with the 4 USD to 1 EOS immediately after its ICO, the value had increased fivefold in only nine months.

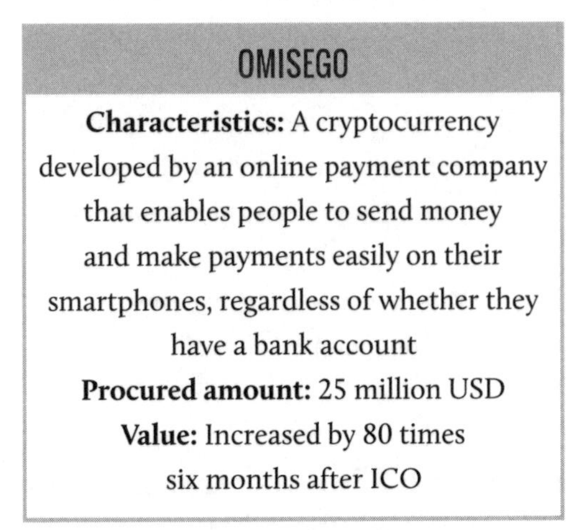
OMISEGO

Characteristics: A cryptocurrency developed by an online payment company that enables people to send money and make payments easily on their smartphones, regardless of whether they have a bank account

Procured amount: 25 million USD

Value: Increased by 80 times six months after ICO

OmiseGO is a cryptocurrency for which 140,245,398 tokens have been issued in total, with the ticker symbol OMG. Developed by a company called omise (which means store in Japanese), a company that includes Japanese investors like the SBI Group and the SMBC Group, OmiseGO is an online payment company that has bases in Thailand, Indonesia and Japan.

OmiseGO's online payments remove the barrier between legal currencies and cryptocurrencies and also enable funds to be sent between mobile terminals. For example, many people in emerging economies do not have a bank account, but OmiseGO is set up to make it easy to send money and make payments in such countries without a bank account. OmiseGO's payment services are particularly well spread in Thailand, and it is said that two-thirds of the mobile companies there use OmiseGO's services. In Thailand, the finance ministry and McDonald's also use OmiseGO.

OmiseGO's ICO was held on 27 June 2017, and transactions began on exchanges on 14 July 2017. OmiseGO's procured funds total 21 million USD; its value had been 0.2738 USD to 10 OMG at its ICO, which became around 10.06 USD to 10 OMG in three months from its 14 July issue. That's around 36 times its initial value.

ARE THERE STORIES OF FAILURES WITH REGARD TO ICOs?

While there are success stories, there are an infinite number of cases of failed ICOs as well, among which an extremely large number are ICOs that were abandoned after they failed to reach development. Approximately 1,000 ICOs failed during the first half of 2018. According to research by the company ICODATA, 1,045 ICOs had taken place by the end of August 2018.[3]

It is important to consider the following before investing in an ICO:

- For some ICOs, neither transfers nor withdrawals may be made
- Some ICOs call for investment with malicious intent
- Scams related to ICOs do occur
- There are cases where it isn't possible to contact the hosts of an ICO
- There have been cases where the host of an ICO was a paper company, a company that is established for the purpose of escaping taxes and transferring debt – only a registered company – and has no substance.

It is better to consider investing with the knowledge that cases like the above exist.

Of the ICOs conducted in the past, 70% of ICOs seem to have issued tokens, but the remaining 30% have not. In only 20% of the ICOs, the investors have earned profits. You aren't likely to know whether the resulting profit will be sufficient to satisfy all investors until at least two or three years have passed.

For example, the cryptocurrency Tezos, with the ticker symbol XTZ, is a large-scale ICO that collected 232.19985 million USD in 2017. In order to resolve the bitcoin division issue, Tezos aimed to become a cryptocurrency that could be updated as specified without a hard fork.

With famous venture capitalists investing in Tezos, there were major expectations for the cryptocurrency. The attempt by Arthur Breitman, the developer and intellectual owner of Tezos, and his wife Kathleen to oust Johann Gevers, president of the Tezos Foundation, triggered an internal dispute within the project. Tokens were not distributed, and no clues could be found to resolve the dispute.

The Tezos Foundation was set up by the Breitmans in Switzerland in order to conduct an ICO for Tezos. (The couple could not become directors at the foundation due to Swiss law on foundations.)

People who had invested in the ICO went on to initiate class-action suits. In October 2017, a lawsuit was filed at the California Superior Court, alleging that the ICO conducted by the Foundation and by Johann Gevers had been unlawful. And in November 2018, Florida investor David Silver filed a class-action lawsuit against the Breitmans.

The gist of the claims was that their actions to collect funds from investors by using donations (the investors' funds were in the form of donations to the foundation, so legally they could not be returned) had been a security issue. This was a violation of US securities law, with investors claiming that: "due to the many misrepresentations, factual omissions and unlawful activities engaged by the defendants – it appears [participants in the ICO] cannot, and potentially will not, see any return on their investments."[4]

Gevers later left the foundation in February 2018 and launched Betanet in June 2018, making it appear that the project had finally regained ground. It is unclear whether the funds invested in the ICO will be returned.

ARE THERE COMMON CAUSES FOR FAILURES?

There are many cases of failed ICOs, as in the previous example. Besides internal disputes, as mentioned above, the chief causes of failure that should be considered are investment scams and inadequate planning.

Disputes occur when interpersonal relationships break down. The cause may be a power struggle or financial trouble, for example. There may also be internal disputes caused by struggles over control concerning whose idea the development was, or differences over which direction the project should take.

Next, there are investment scams, where the party starts out with malicious intent to deceive investors. Huge amounts of money are collected in an ICO: often vast sums of money are collected in a short period, such as 1 million USD or 10 million USD. Naturally, there are people who abuse the capacity to procure such funds.

There seem to be some who make imaginary white papers and prompt investment with skillful words. For example, in an ICO that was conducted at the end of January 2018 by a startup company in Lithuania called Prodeum, the objective was said to be to procure a fund of 6.5 million USD. Although the company disclosed a white paper spanning 12 pages, everything simply disappeared several days after the ICO.

While there was barely any damage when Prodeum disappeared, it was revealed in April 2017 that it had been a scam. In the case of OneCoin, 350 million USD is said to have been stolen.[5]

The Satis Group, a consulting company in the USA specializing in ICOs, has analysed and disclosed information obtained from ICO-related companies and the cryptocurrency information site CoinMarketCap on ICOs that were conducted in 2018.[6] According to the Satis Group's analysis, out of the projects where market capitalization exceeded 50 million USD through an ICO, 81% were scams, 6% suspended operations (failed) before the completion of fund procurement, and 5% did not result in the commencement of cryptocurrency transactions despite procuring funds. Only 4.4% began trading cryptocurrency after procuring funds. Of the whole, 1.9% of ICOs were successful as projects, and about 1.8% could be described as promising.

Inadequate planning basically comes down to an unrealistic business plan. No matter how detailed a plan may be, it is only paper, after all. Anyone can talk. Thus, when considering investing in an ICO, it is necessary to carefully check the history of the people conducting it and their networks to determine whether the plan will take effect.

ARE THERE WAYS TO IDENTIFY ICOs THAT WILL NOT FAIL?

While it is extremely difficult to predict which ICOs will succeed, it is possible to offer percentages for success. In addition to the need to check the business plan and the history and track record of the issuing party, it is also desirable to check the personal character of the issuing party.

In the case of ICOs, a business plan is always disclosed. I suggest that you consider from your own perspective whether the details mentioned are really needed by the world, whether the project may resolve issues in the world, and whether it has the potential for growth.

It may also be important to imagine the situation after the project has been launched – for example, whether you think that life will become more convenient" and it makes your heart flutter. The reason is that an ICO is something that you should invest in based on the level of your expectations.

Checking the history and track record of the issuing party will suggest whether he or she will be able to make the contents of the white paper a reality. No matter how fantastic a plan may be, it is meaningless if it cannot be realized. Checking the person's history and accomplishments will help you evaluate the chances of success.

It is also best to learn as much as you can about the human character of the issuing party. If possible, meet the representative for the issuing party in person. As it is sufficient to conduct procedures concerning cryptocurrency online, face-to-face communications often tend to be neglected. But the fact that an issuing party exists means that the cryptocurrency is run by a company or an organization. In other words, it is no different from investing in a generic business.

If you were investing in a company, you would probably check overviews of the company and maybe visit it, whether you are making an equities investment or a direct investment. Maybe you wouldn't bother to visit if it was a big company that everyone knows about, but at minimum you are likely to check any financial information that is disclosed on the company. You would naturally go and look at property or a building if you were investing in real estate. But when it comes to investing in an ICO or cryptocurrency, these factors tend to be overlooked. Whether the representative is in the country or abroad, you should go and see that person if you have braced yourself to invest.

IS THE DEVELOPMENT OF A CRYPTOCURRENCY THE ONLY OBJECTIVE OF AN ICO?

ICOs were initially a method for procuring funds for developing cryptocurrencies. But they have now also become a method for procuring funds for businesses that have nothing to do with cryptocurrency. In my opinion, this is not a good thing

When starting a new business, funds are often procured through such methods as a loan from a bank or financial institution, investments by investors (private placement bonds or a public issue) or by personal funds.

With a loan from a bank or a financial institution, a business plan is compiled and evidence like a resume, bank book and certificate of income are made available. These documents are taken to the bank for negotiation, then you pay the interest determined by the bank and adhere to the payment period that it decides.

In the case of a company calling for investments from investors, the company issues corporate bonds in the form of private placement bonds or a public issue. While companies often issue private placement bonds, there are also times when a big company that often issues corporate bonds will offer a public issue to make a broad call to investors, appealing to investors about the company's potential, feasibility and growth potential.

Personal funds refer to funds that an individual has made available for his or her business from assets like bank accounts.

For ICOs, which are a method for procuring funds that is similar to issuing corporate bonds, there are few limitations at present on how they're done. For that reason, they're a convenient method for obtaining maximum funding with minimum hassle, and profit sharing for investors may be established freely. In these ways, ICOs are increasingly being used, as they are a convenient way to procure funds.

There are also an increasing number of ICOs associated with the use of blockchain technology, and not particularly for cryptocurrency. These include the development of administration systems for real estate registers and for buying and selling real estate and the development of voting management systems for elections.[7]

An ICO for developing an administration system for a real estate register or for buying and selling property has the potential to bring significant change to the world of real estate. Real estate transactions go through many contractual processes; therefore the procedures are complicated. Since paper contracts are generally used, the process is inefficient and not automated.

By leveraging blockchain and smart contracts, contracts could be made digitally, making it possible to complete all the procedures online and boosting efficiency for tasks like paying funds associated with contracts and for registering real estate. With an ICO for developing a system for a voting management system, for example, it might be possible to complete voting safely and efficiently and proceed with tallying while maintaining anonymity.

An ICO called Boulé became a topic of discussion in 2017. Boulé is a remote voting system (gateway) based on blockchain.

Many countries around the world hold most of their elections offline. When you hear the word election, you probably imagine people marking sheets and putting them in ballot boxes. With Boulé, it was believed that the current methods were old fashioned and that by making it possible to vote online, election activities would become quicker and simpler and tie in to reduced costs. Furthermore, it was also believed that online elections would boost voting rates and tie in to stronger democracy.

Isn't an ICO like Boulé that offers convenience to society and makes it better something that everyone is waiting for? Still, we must not forget that there are also those who will abuse the capacity of ICOs to bring in funds.

CHAPTER 5

BLOWING UP CRYPTOCURRENCY

JUST HOW FAR CAN CRYPTOCURRENCY GO?

While it is difficult to predict the future, I do have a sense that the general value of cryptocurrencies will continue to rise more and more. There should be many cryptocurrencies for which the value will increase tenfold.

With cryptocurrencies, the holders determine and create the value themselves. What becomes important is the extent to which the cryptocurrency that you have is known around the globe. In other words, a boost in a cryptocurrency's level of recognition and convenience will tie in to credibility. Name value and recognition levels will increase if credibility increases, and the level of convenience will further improve through alliances with various companies and services. This is how an upward spiral will occur.

Cryptocurrency market capitalization stood at around 215 USD billion in the middle of August 2018. That said, it is possible to consider continued increases despite minor ups and downs, for which there are a number of reasons.

The first is that the facilitation of laws concerning cryptocurrency should continue to advance in different countries. At the G20 held in March and July 2018, discussions only went so far as to confirm policies for regulations and did not touch on specific details. But if more countries follow Japan, which has facilitated its legislative system a step ahead of the rest of the world, then moves by investors who had been holding back in consideration of the potential for regulations should become invigorated.

Second, the interest in cryptocurrency in developing countries has been boosted. As cryptocurrency is not impacted by a financial collapse of the state or by hyperinflation, it is of high value to societies in countries and regions where the reliability of legal currencies is low. For that reason, an inflow of funds may also be anticipated from developing countries in future.

The third reason for possible increases in the value of cryptocurrencies is that introductions and applications of blockchain technology will be made in various areas. As indicated above, from election management systems to real estate contracts, the possibilities are endless.

HOW FAR CAN BITCOIN GO?

Now, as to individual cryptocurrencies. Taking bitcoins as an example, it is possible to consider that 1 BTC will be worth 100,000 USD.

But as we all know, bitcoin is faced with issues concerning the slow speed of its transfers and the high service charges. Thus, if these issues are resolved, it should significantly increase bitcoin's value as the first cryptocurrency that will continue to boast overwhelming name value and level of convenience.

The tenfold increase is likely because among the numerous cryptocurrencies that exist today, bitcoin has the most advanced facilitation of infrastructure. The advanced facilitation of infrastructure means that it is easy for companies to introduce payments in bitcoins.

In addition, the spread of bitcoin will also impact the dissemination of cryptocurrencies in general, because many altcoins are traded through bitcoin, which is described as a key currency in the world of cryptocurrency. When the value of bitcoin increases, the value of other cryptocurrencies will also increase.

HOW FAR CAN ETHEREUM GO?

It is likely that Ethereum will increase to 5,000 USD to 1 ETH.

In 2018, market capitalization of Ethereum was second to that of bitcoin. Ethereum's position as a symbolic cryptocurrency is unlikely to change in the future. High market capitalization means that trading volume will also be high in proportion. Since symbolic cryptocurrencies like Ethereum are often traded through matches with bitcoin, as mentioned earlier, their movements become coordinated with price fluctuations in bitcoin. Because of that, the chances are high that an increase in the value of bitcoin

HOW FAR CAN RIPPLE GO?

The value of Ripple will rise to 10 USD to 1 XRP.

I asked the following question at an official Ripple forum: "How much will 1 XRP be?" Due to compliance, the response at the time was: "No comment." So I changed my question and asked again: "Would 1 XRP be valued at 1 USD if Ripple took a 10% share of the global market for transactions?" The response was to the effect of: "That's possible, but the Ripple project will be a failure if it can only take 10% market share. Ripple will achieve 70% of the global market."

Ripple is set up in such a way that 0.00001 XRP is destroyed every time that Ripple is used in a transaction. Around the end of 2018, Ripple started to be used for transfers by banks and between financial institutions throughout the world. While the 100 billion coins issued comprise a large number, the more Ripple is used in transactions between banks, the fewer the number of Ripple coins (XRP) there will be, which will cause a relative boost in its value.

Of course, there is a possibility of a delay in Ripple's plans. While it isn't clear when the value will increase, Ripple is one of the cryptocurrencies that is sure to increase in value in five or ten years.

I don't know whether readers of this book will buy when 1 BTC is valued at 10,000 USD or when it is 1 USD to 1 XRP. I don't know how many hundreds of per cent in profit you'll be able to make, either, but if you start buying at an early stage, the chances of you obtaining a profit should increase.

HOW FAR CAN FUSION COIN GO?

I think that the value of Fusion Coin will become 1,000 USD to 1 XFC. This is because, as mentioned above, it has features such as:

- A small number of coins issued
- A fast speed of transfers
- Low handling charges
- Ease in making withdrawals
- A high level of safety

Fusion Coin is also pushing forward projects for boosting its levels of recognition and convenience, by securing privacy, starting the banking business, developing payment apps and by issuing Fusion cards.

The figure 1 XFC at 1,000 USD takes into consideration the prospect that the types of cryptocurrencies that exist will increase in number and the distribution of investments will proceed across the general market. Of course, it is possible that delays will occur and things will not go as planned; however, growth curves are often sudden and rises instantaneous.

Fusion Coin went up about three times during its market launch in 2017, but these are still very low appreciation rates. Its value will continue to increase significantly as long as the release of information on Fusion Coin continues.

The total number of Fusion Coins issued is small at 30 million coins. A small number of issues means a high rate of volatility; boosted recognition and popularity will accelerate the speed of Fusion Coin's increase in value.

Fast speeds of transfer are directly related to high rates of convenience. Fast speeds of transfer mean the processing of payments is fast. While it takes ten minutes on average for bitcoin transfers to be received, a transfer of Fusion Coin is received and completed in a matter of seconds.

Low service charges tie in to convenience as well. Depending on how they are set up, handling charges for transfers of bitcoins are around 0.0001 to 0.001 BTC, but in the case of Fusion Coin the fee is 0.001%. Even if you send 10,000 USD worth of Fusion Coin, the handling fee is only 0.1 USD. At this rate, you barely need to worry, no matter how often you transfer money.

On top of that, Fusion Coin allows withdrawals to be made in Bitcoin, Bitcoin Cash, and Ripple, besides the US dollar. There will be an increase in the types of cryptocurrencies that may be withdrawn in the future. For that reason, the level of convenience should improve.

A high level of safety impacts credibility. No will want to keep their assets at a location where there are fears of hacking. Fusion Coin will continue to strengthen its security and hedge risks with distributed servers and other such steps to protect the assets of its holders. Securing privacy means protecting information on the assets of cryptocurrency holders.

Fusion Coin will start the banking business. As already disclosed, the name will be Fusion Banking. Various financial services are planned to be offered by Fusion Bank.

Fusion Coin is likely to be transformed from one of many cryptocurrencies to a financial services tool. Fusion Partners, which issues Fusion Coin, believes that cooperation with conventional banks is indispensable for boosting credibility and the development of the overall cryptocurrency industry. It is for that purpose that it is moving forward its acquisition of banks that have credibility and history and is setting up new banks in multiple countries and regions.

The smooth connection between cryptocurrency and legal currency will result in boosting the credibility of cryptocurrency. Rather than simply acting as a cryptocurrency exchange, Fusion Bank will handle other cryptocurrencies besides Fusion Coin, as well as legal currency.

Fusion Bank, which is a company that issues cryptocurrency, will become the leader in this field and attract attention and credibility as the first case for owning banks in its corporate umbrella, which, in turn, will tie in to boosted value for Fusion Coin. While cryptocurrency first began as currency that is independent from states and existing financial institutions, it will be detracting for the development of the cryptocurrency industry to continue to be in rivalry with states and financial institutions. Fusion Partners is continuing to take steps with the belief that rather than being in rivalries, it is necessary to fuse the qualities of each. Fusion Partners is a bank that is officially already recognized by the Republic of Malta, and it has also built a cooperative relationship with the government.

The development of payment apps is also underway in Japan. In addition to Fusion Coin, they are also scheduled to be compatible with bitcoin and Bitcoin Cash. To be specific, it will be possible to use Fusion Coin to make a payment on a smartphone or at a store with ease. At present, places like restaurants, jewellery stores, men's clothing stores and beauty salons are considering introducing Fusion Coin.

Plans are also in place to issue Fusion Cards – debit cards for using Fusion Coin. Together with the payment app, the objective will be to increase the use of cryptocurrency payments, because boosted convenience will significantly improve the credibility of cryptocurrency.

Fusion Coin is still a new cryptocurrency, and its name value is not high, but because of that it has the potential for big increases in its value in future. As of 2018, around 20,000 people use Fusion Coin around the world.

On the other hand, according to research by the Cambridge Centre for Alternative Finance, there were three million holders of bitcoins around the world as of 2017.[1] This may appear to be a low estimate, since so many people are already in contact with cryptocurrency and the number is increasing on a daily basis; considerable room still remains for Fusion Coin holders to increase in number. The greater the recognition level of Fusion Coin becomes, the more its value will increase.

CHAPTER 6

THE FUTURE OF CRYPTOCURRENCY

WHAT WILL BE THE POSITION OF CRYPTOCURRENCIES IN THE FUTURE?

Cryptocurrencies are sure to take on a complementary role to legal currencies. To be specific, I think that its use will advance rapidly as a method for sending funds, making payments and making money.

Cryptocurrency is more convenient than legal currency when you're transferring funds or making international transfers. Transfers can be completed instantly with a smartphone. Such use of cryptocurrency is much more convenient compared with the procedures for overseas remittances, where you need to go to the bank and fill out forms, and even for online remittances where you have to enter various pieces of information. Everything from transfers of funds to receipt is possible 24/7, 365 days a year, almost instantaneously.

Although the number of people who use cryptocurrency is still small because of the current low social reliability of cryptocurrency, the number of users should increase in the future.

Payments using cryptocurrency will be highly convenient because cryptocurrency payments are sure to spread in step with the cashless movement. For example, events like the World Cup and the Olympics are opportunities for various types of payment infrastructure within host countries and regions. In addition, after such events, the number of tourists increases and the demand for convenient payment infrastructure that extends beyond the boundaries of legal currencies is strengthened, which is sure to further push the facilitation of such measures.

In 2020, the Olympic Games will be held in Tokyo. In the case of Tokyo, not only tourists but also the inflow of foreigners for business purposes should rapidly increase. Although Japan is behind at present with regard to shifting to a cashless society, things should rapidly move forward after 2020. Payment infrastructure for cryptocurrency may also advance at the same time to achieve the same level of convenience seen in the USA.

The 2022 World Cup (soccer) will be held in Qatar, and the Olympics will be held in Paris in 2024. There is no doubt that global events will serve as opportunities to push the rapid spread of cryptocurrency as a method of payment.

As for making money, the use of cryptocurrency for investment purposes, as seen today, is likely to continue. However, these will not be investments that take a chance in the way of gambling as seen in ICOs; they should become a method for managing assets in a healthy manner. The volatility level will decline, depending on the type of cryptocurrency that is used. Investment in cryptocurrency will probably be seen more in a sense of building your savings rather than making an investment or managing assets.

HOW WILL CRYPTOCURRENCY BE AFFECTED DURING TIMES OF HYPERINFLATION?

As cryptocurrency does not rely on government interest, it is likely to become a currency that temporarily replaces the legal currency should hyperinflation occur.

Many people in Cyprus did not believe that such a situation would happen until the financial crisis occurred in 2013. Some people bought bitcoins to protect their assets, which became a prompt for them to later protect or increase their assets.

The taxing of savings accounts and the cash withdrawal limits have made a huge impact on the daily lives and awareness of people.

The structure of bank savings is established based on the trust relationship between a bank and its depositors. Maintaining a savings account at a bank means that you are entrusting – or lending – your money (or assets) to a bank or financial institution. And in turn, a bank or financial institution increases its revenue by lending to and managing its funds with companies and other parties. It pays back its depositors in the form of interest taken from that revenue. This business model works because of the trust that exists between the bank and its depositors. Trust in local banks and financial institutions hit rock bottom at the time of the financial crisis in Cyprus, and there is no guarantee that the same thing will not happen in another country.

For example, the China shock occurred in June 2015 when investors sold their stocks across the board and the Chinese stock market suddenly crashed. The Dow Jones Industrial Average fell 2,198 USD in a week, and the Nikkei average fell as much as 2,948 yen in a week.

With the SSE Composite Index continuing to more than double in price, which had led the authorities to be wary of soaring prices, there seemed to have been signs of an overheated market, and the crash in China made a huge impact on stock markets around the world. The direct cause is said to have been increasing doubt about China, which had devalued the yuan without warning.

A strong tendency among investors in China seems to be that rather than examining the financial status or business plans of a company, they first invest in a company whose stocks are rising. Because of that, a fall in prices, rather than the future potential or reliability of a company, brings on further uncertainty. An all-out rush to sell stocks to cut back on losses caused the pandemonium. There were investors at the time who directed their assets to cryptocurrencies like bitcoin. Those people were probably able to protect their assets, and they should have managed to increase their assets if they continued to retain them over a long period.

There is concern that a Japan shock could occur to follow the 2008 financial crisis, the Greek debt crisis, the Cypriot financial crisis and the China shock. Japan's national debt continues to be an increasing trend yearly, on top of its decreasing birth rate and the aging of its population. Some experts believe that hyperinflation or default could occur at any time.

In April 2018, the US Department of the Treasury announced that approximately 488 billion USD had been issued in US treasury bonds in the January to March period, a record for a quarter. Meanwhile, it said that demand among foreign investors for US treasury bonds had been at the worst levels since November 2016. If people continue to shy away from US treasury bonds and new bond yields continue to rise, it could lead to a rapid fall in the value of government bonds that have already been issued. Some commentators think that if a massive selling of federal bonds occurs, a grave situation worse than the 2008 financial crisis may occur.[1] The situation will further worsen if China sets out to reduce its US treasury bond purchases due to its trade war with the USA.

In these ways, there are any number of elements of concern in the world that could bring about a blackout in the economic situation. In the event of hyperinflation or an emergency, chances are high that money will flow into cryptocurrency. There are bound to be governments that will recognize that and governments that will not allow that to happen. Depending on the situation, there is also the possibility that governments may confiscate cryptocurrency. Existing banks are controlled by governments. For that reason, there is the possibility of limits being imposed on withdrawals of profit from cryptocurrency or that cryptocurrency might be confiscated. There is a chance that investors in cryptocurrency will not be able to protect their assets unless cryptocurrency service providers have cooperative relationships with governments before something happens.

Therefore, it is eagerly anticipated that a type of presence that connects virtual currency with legal currency, for example a bank that deals with both cryptocurrency and legal currency, will emerge.

WHAT WILL CRYPTOCURRENCY BECOME IN THE FUTURE?

Cryptocurrency will eventually become a method of transferring funds, making payments and making money beyond borders and become a financial asset that comes as close to legal currency as may be imagined. There are probably five hurdles in making such a vision for cryptocurrency of the future a reality, specifically: technical innovations, the reduction of costs, improved reliability, improved usability and improved convenience.

Through technical innovation, the speed of transfers will become even faster. Transactions for transfers that take a few seconds with Ripple or Fusion Coin should be completed instantaneously through improved technology. There was a time in the past when it took several minutes to send a photo by email, but it is now basically possible to do that in an instant. Although it depends on the connection environment, it now takes barely any time to send videos, either. Similar technical innovations and improvements are likely to occur in the world of cryptocurrency as well.

Improved reliability in the context of cryptocurrency refers to the spread of cryptocurrency and improvements in its social credibility. While there are multitudes of types of cryptocurrencies around today, they are bound to be curtailed through project failures and so forth. When scam-like cryptocurrencies and ICOs have been eliminated and people throughout the world have become knowledgeable about individual cryptocurrencies is when trust will improve. The elimination of scam cryptocurrencies should have a huge impact on improving the social status of cryptocurrencies.

Next, cost reduction is needed to reduce remittance fees and trading fees. Although related to technological innovation, further cost reduction is not impossible if cryptocurrency or blockchain with less power consumption can be made.

As for usability, improvements will happen through the easing of limitations on cryptocurrency trading and withdrawals imposed by various governments, regulations regarding privacy, and tax laws. Along with the spread of cryptocurrency and improvements in its social credibility, people's attitudes are bound to make a huge impact on what governments decide to do.

Lastly, regarding the level of convenience, when elimination is complete and the rates of cryptocurrencies become stable, it should become as easy to use cryptocurrencies as it is to use legal currencies. And if the facilitation of payment infrastructure and other such items continues to advance, then cryptocurrencies' level of convenience will further improve.

On the other hand, new cryptocurrencies that involve innovative technology are likely to have high rates of volatility for investing. Technical innovation may occur in any industry and in any era.

If a discerning eye is used, it is certainly possible to invest in a new cryptocurrency and increase your assets, even after cryptocurrencies have become more widespread.

CONCLUSION

THE FUTURE OF CRYPTOCURRENCY IN THE CHANGING WORLD

Our economic life has long been in a stage where we cannot stand by just 'legal currency'. Alternative payment instruments such as electronic money have overwhelmingly facilitated daily life, and cashless settlement methods have expanded at overwhelming speed and scale, even at the level of international transactions between companies.

In that context, the birth of 'encryption currency' was inevitable. Moreover, because strong security is guaranteed by blockchain technology, it is natural that other alternative payment methods will be overshadowed.

As long as a nation state with sovereignty survives, cryptocurrency will not replace or surpass legal currency. However, cryptocurrency supplements legal currencies and cannot be separated from every economic activity.

Nevertheless, cryptocurrency will develop mainly in three respects: technical aspects, legal aspects and social credibility.

First of all, technical aspects refer to the technology that supports the encryption currency, based on the blockchain. A cryptographic currency that realizes more speedy payment and remittance, further cost reduction and stronger security might appear.

Next, legal aspects refer to legislation concerning the cryptocurrency of each country, which is not yet complete. However, if legislation in each country progresses, those who were more cautious about cryptocurrency might enter the market.

Of course, it is also possible that the movement of the market will slow down as legislative developments proceed. Nevertheless, many people will think that it is safer to have laws. Once laws are in place, cryptocurrency fraud and scam ICO projects should be eliminated. Elimination of fraudulent encryption currency and ICO projects is a welcome situation for all cryptocurrency, which will foster the final aspect, social credibility.

Currently only the speculative side is being futuristic, but if awareness and social credibility increase, the range of uses in settlement use, remittance use and so on will be widened significantly. In that case, the demand for the new era of financial services that integrates current banking services and encryption currency will also be greatly increased. I believe it will become the standard of financial services in the near future.

As development progresses in various aspects like this, only those cryptocurrencies that are truly safe and have high functions will remain. Cryptocurrency is in transition, but there is dynamism unique to the transition period. There is a possibility of immeasurable developments emerging. What is necessary is the ability to accurately determine the encryption currency that is necessary in the changing world.

While our world has already reached a point where it cannot be separated from the cryptocurrency, it is rapidly changing further with the cryptocurrency.

EPILOGUE: THE FUTURE OF FUSION COIN

THE FUTURE OF CRYPTOCURRENCY AS ENVISIONED BY FUSION PARTNERS

By establishing Fusion Bank, which is planned in 2019, Fusion Partners will shape a platform for the free administration of assets that leverages cryptocurrency. Free, here, has four meanings: fast money transfer, low handling charges, liberation from limitations on deposits and withdrawals, and the securing of privacy.

The speed of money transfers is so high that you can send money in a matter of seconds, regardless of whether the destination is in your country or abroad. It is possible to send money in no time, even to the other side of the planet. There is no need to worry about the days or hours that banks are open, either. You can send as much as you want, when you want, to the person you want to send money to. That may seem like a natural thing to want to do, but it is not all that easy in real life.

Barely any service charges are applied. The handling fee is only 0.1 USD, even if you send 10,000 USD worth of coins. It's an amount that would cause little concern and allows you to send money at your leisure. There's no need to pay high service charges anymore.

There are no annoying limitations on how much you can deposit or withdraw, either. You can deposit as much as you want and you can withdraw as much as you want.

Furthermore, your privacy is secured and there is no need to worry that information on your assets may be leaked. This is because the security level is high and safety is secured.

Fusion Bank should be able to meet the needs of various people, including:

- People who feel secure by having cryptocurrency
- People who feel secure by having legal currency
- People who feel secure by having real assets

The banking arm, Fusion Bank, handles both cryptocurrency and legal currency and makes it possible to exchange various cryptocurrencies to legal currency. In addition to enabling exchanges to real assets like gold and silver, it will proceed to make preparations for further exchanges with other assets.

Fusion Bank also plans to start offering loans with cryptocurrency and with cryptocurrency as collateral. As it is possible to make exchanges to legal currencies like the dollar, the euro and the yen, it should no longer be necessary to use cryptocurrency exchanges with high service charges if you use Fusion Bank's services.

For these reasons, the presence of Fusion Bank should make a huge impact on the world of cryptocurrency and that of finance and further continue to extend its influence.

FUSION PARTNERS' ROAD MAP

Fusion Partners revealed a road map in June 2018 and announced banking initiatives, including the acceptance of deposits and lending, the development of payment app(s), the issuing of debit cards, the development of a mobile wallet, mobile app(s) and a mobile banking system, and collaborations with cryptocurrency exchanges.

SHOW FUSION PARTNERS' ROAD MAP

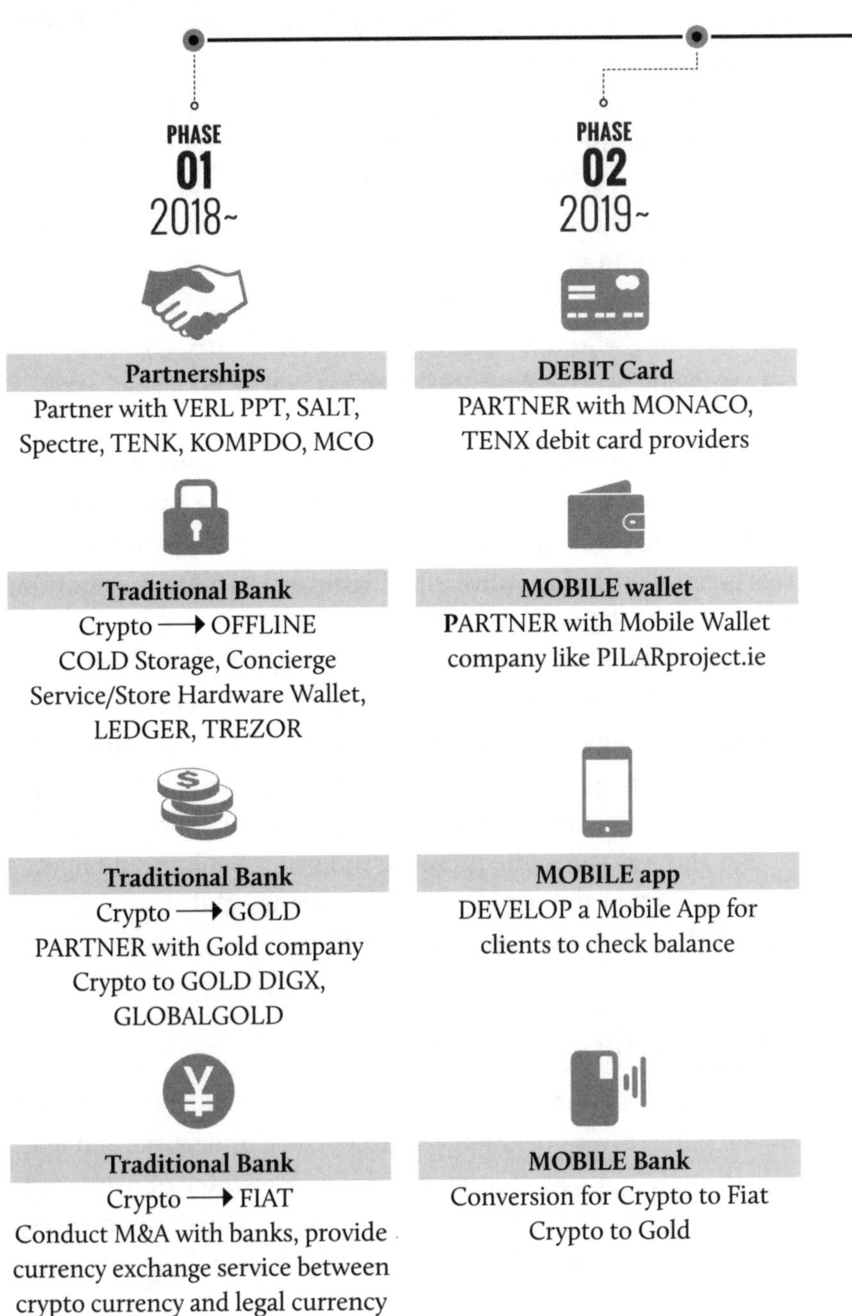

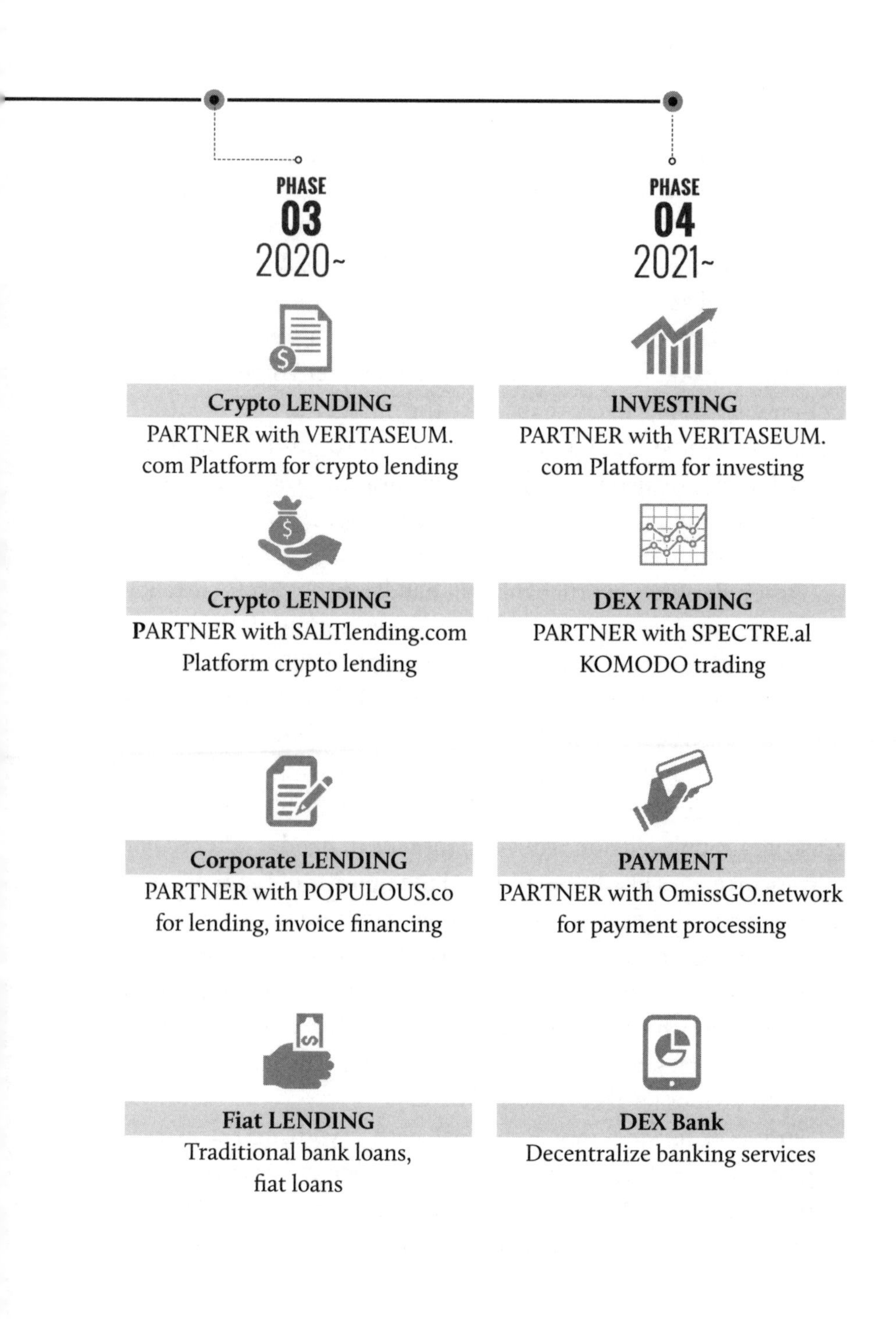
PHASE
03
2020~
PHASE
04
2021~
Crypto LENDING
PARTNER with VERITASEUM.
com Platform for crypto lending
INVESTING
PARTNER with VERITASEUM.
com Platform for investing
Crypto LENDING
PARTNER with SALTlending.com
Platform crypto lending
DEX TRADING
PARTNER with SPECTRE.al
KOMODO trading
Corporate LENDING
PARTNER with POPULOUS.co
for lending, invoice financing
PAYMENT
PARTNER with OmissGO.network
for payment processing
Fiat LENDING
Traditional bank loans,
fiat loans
DEX Bank
Decentralize banking services

The more details on its road map are made to happen, the more the value of Fusion Coin will increase. Incidentally, the road map will continue to be updated. For the latest version, please see Fusion Partners' official website at http://fusioncoin.info/trajectory.

Regardless of their ethnicity or nationality, anyone in the world can use Fusion Bank and Fusion Coin, because the company aims to open banks in many countries and regions to realize highly reliable financial services that ensure safety and privacy.

Fusion Bank and Fusion Coin will become a hub, bring people together and create a community. The strengthening of the community will be likely to increase the number of fans of Fusion Bank and Fusion Coin and serve as an aid to push forward the spread of cryptocurrency in general in various ways – for making payments, sending money and for making money in all countries of the world.

Fusion Bank is a hybrid bank that handles both cryptocurrency and legal currency. Tying together the innovation of cryptocurrencies with existing banks and legal currencies will boost the credibility and status of cryptocurrency and initiate financial services that are safe and offer high credibility in all parts of the globe.

Besides dealing with Fusion Coin, Fusion Bank also handles other cryptocurrencies. Specifically, these include bitcoin, Bitcoin Cash and Ripple. Fusion Bank also intends to handle other major cryptocurrencies like Ethereum, and the number of types of cryptocurrencies it deals with should increase in future.

As for legal currencies, Fusion Bank deals with the US dollar and the euro, as well as currencies like the yen. By accessing Fusion Bank, it is possible to exchange a cryptocurrency to various other cryptocurrencies, and it is also possible to exchange a cryptocurrency to various legal currencies.

Fusion Bank does not only deal with cryptocurrencies and legal currencies. It is also possible to exchange cryptocurrency to real assets like gold and silver. Gold, in particular, continues to enjoy deep-rooted popularity. There is no need to hold assets only in cryptocurrency or legal currency. Fusion Bank hopes that investors will leverage various assets to build their portfolios.

Fusion Bank is not just online, as it operates physical banks in Britain. The operation of physical banks should further enhance the credibility of Fusion Bank, which should tie in to boosting the credibility of the cryptocurrency industry as a whole.

Alliances between Fusion Bank and various companies and organizations were announced in 2018, including with the cryptocurrencies SALT, Spectre, TenX, Komodo and Monaco:

- SALT (Secured Automated Lending Technology), a cryptocurrency with 120 million coins issued, became public in August 2017.

  A SALT holder is able to receive loans in legal currency when needed without having to exchange cryptocurrency to legal currency. As of 2018, the cryptocurrencies that may be used as collateral are bitcoin, Ethereum and Ripple, and there are plans for other cryptocurrencies like Fusion Coin to be added in the future.
- Spectre (SpectreCoin) is a cryptocurrency with the ticker symbol XSPEC. In November 2016, 20 million coins were issued. Spectre is a cryptocurrency that has a high level of anonymity and privacy. It uses Smart Contracts on the Ethereum blockchain and operates a decentralized prediction market platform for predicting price fluctuations in legal currencies and other currencies to make a profit. Essentially this is a structure in which participants bet money on future events and what they think will happen, and those who make the correct predictions are able to obtain remuneration. Smart Contracts execute the structure automatically.

  The advantage of a decentralized prediction market platform is the increased level of accuracy and transparency in market predictions. If brokers are eliminated, it becomes possible to remove the types of uncertainty that accompany binary options and FX trading. In centralized markets where brokers exist, there is room for wrongful conduct by brokers, like price manipulation. It should be possible to remove conflicts of interest by using blockchains and by eliminating brokers.

- TenX is a cryptocurrency that went public in June 2016 with 252.18256 million coins issued, and its units are PAY. TenX issues cryptocurrency debit cards that were the first to allow cards and wallets to be tied together for use. While there had been cards that moved currency from wallets for use, a characteristic of TenX is that currency may be left in a wallet and used for payments. The money is automatically exchanged to legal currency immediately before payment and then withdrawn.
- Komodo's ticker symbol is KMD, and 200 million coins were issued when it was made public in September 2016. It uses technology called Atomic Swaps and allows users who have cryptocurrencies with different blockchains to conduct transactions directly, without the need to go through an exchange, and therefore also to save on the service charge. In total there are 32 legal currencies that Komodo can be exchanged with. Komodo may become a cryptocurrency like Fusion Coin and connect cryptocurrency with legal currency.
- Monaco went public in May 2017 with a total 315.87682 million coins issued, and its ticker symbol is MCO. It was issued by Monaco, a credit card company based in Hong Kong, and it enables debit card payments to be made using cryptocurrency.

  A major feature of Monaco is that multiple cryptocurrencies may be stored in a Monaco account, and withdrawals may be made throughout the world without handling charges being incurred. Monaco uses a credit card platform, and you can make cash deposits, exchange Monaco to other cryptocurrencies, send money, or make payments with the debit card using cryptocurrency.

The convenience level of Fusion Coin should improve dramatically through alliances with various companies or organizations that issue or operate cryptocurrency.

Fusion Bank has cold wallets that allow you to store cryptocurrency offline, hardware wallets, and concierge services that administer them, through alliances with Ledger and Trezor, which make hardware wallets.

Fusion Bank also has alliances with Digix, which administers the ownership of gold on a blockchain, and Global Gold, and it is possible to exchange cryptocurrencies like Fusion Coin to other real assets like gold. Of course, it is also possible to conduct transactions between cryptocurrency and legal currency at Fusion Bank.

In 2019, Fusion Bank will issue debit cards in collaboration with TenX and Monaco and also develop a mobile app for checking balances and also mobile banking that enables transactions of cryptocurrency and legal currency.

In 2020, Fusion Bank will start a financial service that will include cryptocurrency loans in collaboration with SALT and other parties and corporate financing. Through such deployments, Fusion Bank will offer various services around the globe in 2021, which will include the development of an investment platform, the establishment of a decentralized cryptocurrency exchange in alliance with Spectre and Komodo, and the development of a payment system in collaboration with OmiseGO.

The existence of Fusion Coin should contribute to boosting the credibility of the overall cryptocurrency industry and promote its dissemination.

ENDNOTES

CHAPTER 1

1 There are some cryptocurrencies like Ethereum that may continue to be issued without limit. They are sometimes called 'inflation currency', versus 'deflation currency' where the number of issues is limited.

2 The implied volatility rate of a financial instrument. The higher the volatility, the greater the fluctuation of the prices will be. Reverse when low.

3 https://www.nbcnews.com/tech/tech-news/bitcoin-breakthrough-cryptocurrency-welcome-zug-switzerland-n571921

4 "A Guide to 'Monetary Base and the Bank of Japan's Transactions'," Policy Planning Office, Bank of Japan, 8 June 2000, https://www.boj.or.jp/en/statistics/outline/exp/data/exmbt01.pdf

5 FindLaw, "California Code, Corporations Code - CORP § 29100," https://codes.findlaw.com/ca/corporations-code/corp-sect-29100.html

6 Washington State Legislature, "Bucket shop defined," RCW 9.47.080, http://apps.leg.wa.gov/RCW/default.aspx?cite=9.47.080

7 babypips, "Beware of Forex Bucket Shops," https://www.babypips.com/learn/forex/beware-of-bucket-shops

Ayan Brahmachary, "What is a Forex Bucket Shop? How You Can Identify Bucket Shops?," Finance Origin, 19 April 2018, https://www.financeorigin.com/forex-bucket-shop

8 Das, S., "BitLicense #7: New York Grants Another License to Bitcoin App Square," ccn, 18 June 2018, https://www.ccn.com/bitlicense-7-new-york-grants-another-license-to-bitcoin-app-square/

9 Dhaliwal, S., "BlockShow Announces BlockShow Americas 2018 Conference in Las Vegas August 20-21," cointelegraph, 21 July 2018, https://cointelegraph.com/news/blockshow-announces-blockshow-americas-2018-conference-in-las-vegas-august-20-21

10 Financial Conduct Authority (FCA), "Cryptocurrency derivatives," "FCA statement on the requirement for firms offering cryptocurrency derivatives to be authorised," 6 April 2018, https://www.fca.org.uk/news/statements/cryptocurrency-derivatives

11 Ibid.

12 Coleman, L., "UK Financial Regulator Launches 24 Cryptocurrency Investigations," ccn, 30 May 2018, https://www.ccn.com/uk-financial-regulator-launches-24-cryptocurrency-investigations/

13 Helms, K., "Russia Finalizes Federal Law on Cryptocurrency Regulation," Bitcoin.com, 26 January 2018, https://news.bitcoin.com/russia-finalizes-federal-law-cryptocurrency-regulation/

14 Money that is not backed by money metal such as gold.

15 Buck, J., "Russian Ministry of Finance to Legalize Cryptocurrency Trading on Approved Exchanges," cointelegraph, 13 January 2018, https://cointelegraph.com/news/russian-ministry-of-finance-to-legalize-cryptocurrency-trading-on-approved-exchanges

16 BitcoinExchangeGuide, "New Russian Regulations Replace 'Cryptocurrency' with 'Digital Rights' Terminology" 14 June 2018, https://bitcoinexchangeguide.com/new-russian-regulations-replace-cryptocurrency-with-digital-rights-terminology/

17 Helms, K., "Hong Kong Cracks Down on Securities Tokens – 7 Crypto Exchanges Targeted" Bitcoin.com, 9 February 2018, https://news.bitcoin.com/hong-kong-cracks-down-securities-tokens-cryptocurrency-exchanges/

18 Ibid.

19 Reuters, "Singapore explores rules to protect investors in cryptocurrencies," 1 March 2018, https://www.reuters.com/article/us-singapore-cryptocurrency/singapore-looking-at-investor-protection-rules-for-cryptocurrencies-idUSKCN1GD3OL

20 A negative handling fee means that the amount equivalent to the handling fee for a specific transaction will be accepted when that transaction is conducted.

21 A character string calculated from the private keys.

22 Public keys cannot be opened or decrypted without using the correct private keys.

23 The act of placing an order without designating the price.

CHAPTER 2

1 Nakamoto, S., "Bitcoin: A Peer-to-Peer Electronic Cash System," bitcoin, https://bitcoin.org/bitcoin.pdf

2 This is what the general participants in the network that supports the framework of Bitcoins are called.

3 An academic mailing list that specializes in cryptography.

4 Called Bitcoin Forum, Bitcointalk and also abbreviated as BCT.

5 Popper, N., *Digital Gold: Bitcoin and the Inside Story of the Misfits and Millionaires Trying to Reinvent Money* (Nikkei Publishing Inc., 2015), p.80.

6 Popper, N., *Digital Gold: Bitcoin and the Inside Story of the Misfits and Millionaires Trying to Reinvent Money* (Nikkei Publishing Inc., 2015), p.104.

7 Jeffries, A., "FBI: That Bitcoin Report Was Authentic, But It Wasn't Leaked by Us," *Observer*, 14 May 2012, http://observer.com/2012/05/fbi-that-bitcoin-report-was-authentic-but-it-wasnt-leaked-by-us

FBI, "Bitcoin Virtual Currency: Unique Features Present Distinct Challenges for Deterring Illicit Activity," 24 April 2012, https://www.wired.com/images_blogs/threatlevel/2012/05/Bitcoin-FBI.pdf

8 Santori, M., "What New York's Proposed Regulations Mean for Bitcoin Businesses" coindesk, 18 July 2014, https://www.coindesk.com/new-yorks-proposed-regulations-mean-bitcoin-businesses

9 Bello Perez, Y., "Bitcoin Is Exempt from VAT, Rules European Court of Justice," coindesk, 22 October 2015, https://www.coindesk.com/bitcoin-is-exempt-from-vat-says-european-court-of-justice

10 The Economist, "The promise of the blockchain: The trust machine," 31 October 2015, https://www.economist.com/leaders/2015/10/31/the-trust-machine

11 Hearn, M., "The resolution of the Bitcoin experiment," Mike's blog, 14 January 2016, https://blog.plan99.net/the-resolution-of-the-bitcoin-experiment-dabb30201f7

12 Coleman, L., "Japan Accepts Bitcoin as Legal Payment Method. What's Next?" ccn, 5 April 2014, https://www.ccn.com/japan-accepts-bitcoin-as-legal-payment-method-whats-next

13 The Asahi Shimbun, "Japan penalizes cryptocurrency exchanges after hack" The Associated Press, 8 March 2018, http://www.asahi.com/ajw/articles/AJ201803080086.html

14 Mizrahi, A., "Bitcoin and Cryptocurrencies Are Commodities, Federal Court Rules," Bitcoin.com, 7 March 2018, https://news.bitcoin.com/bitcoin-cryptocurrencies-commodities-federal-court-rules/?utm_source=OneSignal%20Push&utm_medium=notification&utm_campaign=Push%20Notifications

15 Mizrahi, A., "Bitcoin and Cryptocurrencies Are Commodities, Federal Court Rules," Bitcoin.com, 7 March 2018, https://news.bitcoin.com/bitcoin-cryptocurrencies-commodities-federal-court-rules/?utm_source=OneSignal%20Push&utm_medium=notification&utm_campaign=Push%20Notifications

16 Küster, F., "Lohnt Sich Bitcoin Mining Noch in 2019?" *Die Kryptozeitung*, https://tokenthusiast.com/2018/04/10/bitcoin-industry-steals-top-talent-from-banks-and-tech-companies

17 An independent organization recognized by the Swiss government that was set up to establish a region in Zug, a municipality in Switzerland, as a base for global blockchains and encryption systems.

18 Kasanmascheff, M., "PwC Report Finds That 2018 ICO Volume is Already Double That of Previous Year," cointelegraph, 30 June 2018, https://cointelegraph.com/news/pwc-report-finds-that-2018-ico-volume-is-already-double-that-of-previous-year

CHAPTER 3

1 A currency that is used widely for settlements in international financial transactions.

2 Fugger, R., "Money as IOUs in Social Trust Networks & A Proposal for a Decentralized Currency Network Protocol," 18 April 2004, http://archive.ripple-project.org/decentralizedcurrency.pdf

3 Ripple, http://gtgox.com/partners-of-ripple/#i-2

4 Althauser, J., "Washington State Requires Bitcoin Exchanges to Secure Licenses," cointelegraph, 28 July 2017, https://cointelegraph.com/news/washington-state-requires-bitcoin-exchanges-to-secure-licenses

5 Micklethwait, J., Ross, T. and Ward, J., "May Says She'll Look 'Very Seriously' at Action on Bitcoin," Bloomberg, 25 January 2018, https://www.bloomberg.com/news/articles/2018-01-25/u-k-s-may-will-look-very-seriously-at-action-on-bitcoin

6 Redman, J., "France Appoints a Cryptocurrency 'Mission Leader'," Bitcoin.com, 16 January 2018, https://news.bitcoin.com/france-appoints-a-cryptocurrency-mission-leader

7 Le Maire, B., "Tribune: Cryptoactifs, blockchain & ICO: comment la France veut rester à la pointe, par Bruno Le Maire," *numerama*, 19 March 2018, https://www.numerama.com/politique/336943-tribune-cryptoactifs-blockchain-ico-comment-la-france-veut-rester-a-la-pointe-par-bruno-le-maire.html

Esteves, R., "France Regulates Cryptocurrencies to Build 'The World of Tomorrow'," NewsBTC, 22 March 2018, https://www.newsbtc.com/2018/03/22/france-regulates-cryptocurrencies-to-build-the-world-of-tomorrow

8 Suberg, W., "Major Swiss Online Bank Unleashes Bitcoin In Week's Second Swiss Breakthrough," cointelegraph, 14 July 2017, https://cointelegraph.com/news/major-swiss-online-bank-unleashes-bitcoin-in-weeks-second-swiss-breakthrough

9 Securities and Futures Commission (SFC), "SFC warns of cryptocurrency risks," 9 February 2018, https://www.sfc.hk/edistributionWeb/gateway/EN/news-and-announcements/news/doc?refNo=18PR13

10 A framework to collect funds from a number of investors to conduct business/to invest, and to distribute profits to the investors.

11 Securities and Futures Commission (SFC), "SFC's regulatory action halts ICO to Hong Kong public," 19 March 2018, https://www.sfc.hk/edistributionWeb/gateway/EN/news-and-announcements/news/doc?refNo=18PR29

12 Mu-Hyun, C., "South Korea bans digital currency offerings," ZDNet, 29 September 2017, https://www.zdnet.com/article/south-korea-bans-digital-currency-offerings

13 Reuters, "Brazil regulator bans funds from buying cryptocurrencies," 12 January 2018, https://www.reuters.com/article/brazil-bitcoin/brazil-regulator-bans-funds-from-buying-cryptocurrencies-idUSL1N1P71DV

14 https://www.cb.is/publications-news-and-speeches/news-and-speeches/news/2014/03/19/Significant-risk-attached-to-use-of-virtual-currency

15 Tatar, J., "Iceland—Time to Free Bitcoin!" *the balance*, 15 December 2018, https://www.thebalance.com/iceland-time-to-free-bitcoin-4030896

16 Zuckerman, M. J., "Iceland: Crypto Mining Companies Will Consume More Energy Than Households In 2018," cointelegraph, 12 February 2018, https://cointelegraph.com/news/iceland-crypto-mining-companies-will-consume-more-energy-than-households-in-2018

17 The Law Library of Congress, "Regulation of Cryptocurrency Around the World," June 2018, https://www.loc.gov/law/help/cryptocurrency/cryptocurrency-world-survey.pdf

18 Internal Revenue Service (IRS), Notice 2014-21, https://www.irs.gov/pub/irs-drop/n-14-21.pdf

19 HM Revenue & Customs, "Revenue and Customs Brief 9 (2014): Bitcoin and other cryptocurrencies" policy paper, 3 March 2014, https://www.gov.uk/government/publications/revenue-and-customs-brief-9-2014-bitcoin-and-other-cryptocurrencies/revenue-and-customs-brief-9-2014-bitcoin-and-other-cryptocurrencies

20 Zuckerman, M. J., "France: Crypto Is Now 'Moveable Property', Tax Down From 45 To 19 Percent," cointelegraph, 27 April 2018, https://cointelegraph.com/news/france-crypto-is-now-moveable-property-tax-down-from-45-to-19-percent

21 Tokens 24, "Cryptocurrency Tax Rate Stands At 13% in Russia," 1 April 2018, https://www.tokens24.com/news/cryptocurrency-tax-rate-stands-13-russia

22 A framework to calculate the tax rate as a total with other income.

23 The Brazil Business, "Taxation on Bitcoin," http://thebrazilbusiness.com/article/taxation-on-bitcoin

CHAPTER 4

1 Bonds that are issued to a small number of designated investors.

2 Jeff Walker has published a book entitled *Launch*.

3 ICODATA.IO, "Funds raised in 2018," https://www.icodata.io/stats/2018

4 Bakies, L., "Tezos is Being Sued (Again) in a Class Action Lawsuit," *CryptoCoinMastery*, 16 November 2017, https://cryptocoinmastery.com/tezos-sued-class-action-lawsuit

5 Matsakis, L., "cryptocurrency scams are just straight-up trolling at this point," Wired, 30 January 2018, https://www.wired.com/story/cryptocurrency-scams-ico-trolling

6 Wasik, J., "Are Most Digital Coin Offerings Scams?," *Forbes*, 23 April 2018, https://www.forbes.com/sites/johnwasik/2018/04/23/are-most-digital-coin-offerings-scams/#bd1b03f256d1

Wang, B., "Overall ICOs raising more money in 2018 but the failure and scam rate is high," NextBigFuture.com, 5 April 2018, https://www.nextbigfuture.com/2018/04/overall-icos-raising-more-money-in-2018-but-the-failure-and-scam-rate-is-high.html

7 Zilbert, M., "The Blockchain For Real Estate, Explained," *Forbes*, 23 April 2018, https://www.forbes.com/sites/forbesrealestatecouncil/2018/04/23/the-blockchain-for-real-estate-explained/#4e31808a781e

CHAPTER 5

1 University of Cambridge, "Study highlights growing significance of cryptocurrencies," 4 May 2017, https://www.cam.ac.uk/research/news/study-highlights-growing-significance-of-cryptocurrencies

CHAPTER 6

1 Goodkind, N., "U.S. debt is growing and foreigners are buying less: here's why that could be disastrous for the economy," *Newsweek*, 2 May 2018, https://www.newsweek.com/trump-tax-cuts-debt-china-907763

ABOUT THE AUTHOR

Joe McKenzie is a fictional character. He is a combination of the founder, CEO and management team at Fusion Partners, which issues Fusion Coin. They have been involved in the industry since the inception of cryptocurrency and have been spreading cryptocurrency in general. Their dissemination activities include the establishment of bitcoin ATMs, enlightenment for Ripple, and sales. They became acquainted with one another through business and personal interests.

They developed a Fusion Coin as a more convenient next generation cryptocurrency. And, with the vision of providing highly reliable financial services and connecting people so that everyone in the world can access it, the Fusion Bank will be opened. With blockchain technology, they are introducing innovative technologies in traditional banking systems, aiming to provide global, safe and reliable financial services.